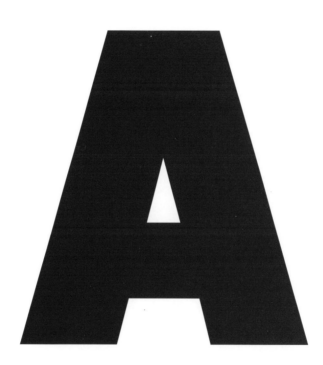

BRANDS A TO Z: ALESSI
Copyright © 2009 PAGE ONE PUBLISHING PTE LTD

Published in 2009 by
Page One Publishing Pte Ltd
20 Kaki Bukit View
Kaki Bukit Techpark II
Singapore 415956
Tel: (65) 6742 2088
Fax: (65) 6744 2088
enquiries@pageonegroup.com
www.pageonegroup.com

Art Direction & Design: Frédéric Snauwaert
Editors: Adeline Loh, Wong She-reen and Crystal Lee
Copy Editor: Melody Tan

Typeset in *ITC Slimbach*, *Univers* and *Euphemia UCAS*

ISBN 978-981-245-862-9

Printed and bound by:
Dami Editorial & Printing Services Co. Ltd

ALESSI

LEARNING
RESOURCES
CENTRE

CONTENTS

INTRODUCTION

Claus Sendlinger stands in front of a blown up image of an odd-looking metal contraption that very much resembles an arachnidan creature from space. He looks around amongst the audience and asks if anyone recognises it. Almost the entire room nods or replies in the affirmative. The president of Design Hotels™ has just started his presentation in Singapore on the cultural relevance and value of design. Philippe Starck's Juicy Salif for Alessi was picked for the opening slide because it epitomised a product that was a design icon, that was highly desirable and collectible, and which spoke to people on an emotional, associative level. Furthermore the fact that it was so instantly recognisable is an indicator of the position Alessi occupies in culture, far beyond the confines of the kitchen and the domestic. The popularity of the Anna G., the La Conica espresso coffee maker, or the kettle with a bird perched on its spout that was an icon in the 1980s, testify to the profound way the brand has permeated our everyday lives. Witness its cameo appearances in popular mainstream films. Michael Graves' pepper mill in *The Matrix*. *Sex and the City*'s wire basket. The 9093 kettle with a bird-shaped whistle in *Ghost*. Wine coolers, cocktail shakers and hors d'œuvre sets in *Ocean's Twelve*. The appearances of the Juicy Salif in movies are countless.

Hollywood's love affair with Alessi kitchenware is representative of a wider cultural phenomenon. This is the same trend that saw the Juicy Salif taking pride of place in the sleek stainless steel-dominated kitchens of yuppies in the 1980s and becoming a highly-coveted design item on wedding registries. Today, the ardour for all things Alessi has not abated. To use film as a cultural indicator again, the recent Hollywood offering, *Confessions of a Shopaholic* includes a scene shot in Alessi's flagship store in Soho, New York, where the lead character Rebecca goes crazy over the merchandise.

The company recognises their position in popular culture only too well, and has responded decisively in a shrewd marketing move. In 2006, it organised its vast catalogue of products in a tripartite division: Alessi, Officina Alessi and A di Alessi. The first is the traditional brand originated from Omegna, which underwent a radical structural change in the 1950s and 60s with the adoption of steel as dominant material, leading to the Italian firm becoming one of the key players in the industry in the decades to come. Officina Alessi comprises the crème de la crème in the company's stable: limited edition items set at a premium price point. More crucially, they are free from the limits of mass production, allowing commissioned designers a playground for experimentation and innovation. The last branch of the brand is, on a surface level, the most lightweight and trivial of the three, pitched price and design-wise for the populace. Yet initiatives such as Family Follows Fiction reveal the more careful and serious philosophical thought on which these seemingly toy-like products are modelled. Such is the Janus-faced aspect of Alessi. On the one hand, its playful frivolity and willingness to use its branding in tongue-in-cheek ways – it is safe to assume that not many companies would photograph their chairman with a water hose in a stance mimicking going to the toilet – on the other, the critical theorising of the value and relevance of design and the applied arts, as well as the undertaking of publications dedicated to expounding design philosophy. This willingness to spend effort and resources on research underscores the trait that sets Alessi apart from other commercial enterprises, and the direction under Alberto Alessi which the firm has taken. This course is the principle of what Alberto calls the "borderline", the factory that is "heroic" in its endeavour, a role that has produced items which are highly innovative, experimental and formally complex, and which have also cost the company dearly. Which is the whole point. Alessi is famous for the leeway it gives to designers: the tolerance and celebration of products that fail in one way or other, but which embody creative possibilities (what Alessi calls "poetic value") so cherished by the company. These "fiascos", Alberto maintains, with regard to the output of the business he runs, are so imperative to the identity of Alessi that "the rest of the family starts to be concerned if in one year I do not practice at least one fiasco: it would mean that we are losing our leading position in design excellence."

Brands A to Z: Alessi pays tribute to this core tenet – and Alberto's favourite mistakes – with a section on design fiascos, showcasing amongst others, the famous Howitzer-shaped Hot Bertaa water kettle, which was nearly impossible to handle. Honouring Alessi's commitment to creative possibility, this book also contains a chapter called 'Dreaming Out Loud', which includes unreleased prototypes and experimental projects which may or may not have been manufactured. This book comes at a time that nearly coincides with the release of several new lines of products, including OrienTales, the tableware line modelled after colourful fish, birds and monkeys and the Miniatures, palm-sized versions of Alessi bestsellers. Within the year, the Alessi Shop Museum designed by Martí Guixé opens in Paris, with playful doodles covering its walls and glass front.

Alessi has come a long way from its beginnings as a tableware company manufacturing in brass and nickel silver in 1921. In the 21st century, it is exploring avenues and producing items that speak to the more intimate, domestic, even child-like aspects of people. Metal products remain its core dealing, but the approach is fresher, younger and more modern, as seen in the design of the Paris store. This is the same approach that *Brands A to Z: Alessi* has taken in its conceptualisation and delivery. It is part of a legacy, a bequest to the future of the Italian design factory. Alberto calls the kitchen a "temple of domestic creativity" while Alessandro Mendini, the company's designer, architect, historian and family friend, talks about a "poetic kitchen". It seems only metaphors will suffice when it comes to products that derive from, spark off ideas in, and ultimately belong to, the realm of *poiesis*.

SETTING THE STAGE

The Story of Alessi

HISTORY

One of the most often-quoted lines from the Modernist writer T.S. Eliot is not from one of his poems or plays. It is from his most important piece of criticism, 'Tradition and the Individual Talent', where he explains what he means by a historical sense: "[…] the historical sense involves a perception, not only of the pastness of the past, but of its presence". This sense of being an inheritor of a tradition is felt not just with regard to "his own generation in his bones", but of something larger, and which renders the individual "most acutely conscious of his place in time, of his contemporaneity." While Eliot was specifically referring to writers, the quote is significant because it has been taken as representative of the ethos of the Modernist movement in literature and other arts, articulating the apocalyptic sense of crisis facing the world still reeling from the first world war it has ever seen.

The publication of the essay in 1919 almost coincides with another event that is more immediately relevant to our purposes: in the aftermath of the war, Giovanni Alessi started the Alessi company in Omegna near Lake Orta in the Italian alps bordering Switzerland, in 1921. This narrow, impoverished valley with a rich heritage of wood and metal handicraft was the setting for Giovanni to establish his officina, his workshop producing tableware in brass plated in nickel, chrome and silver. His grandson Alberto's famous declaration that "Alessi products are still considered as handicraft made with the aid of machines" is an allusion to this artisan heritage. Yet even in 1921, the region could already look back on more than 200 years of history in craftsmanship, dating from the 17th century when some of its people migrated to Westphalia in Germany to learn pewter manufacture. Those who came back set up their own factories in metal household appliances. The industry in the region blossomed and workshops producing items in nickel silver, brass, copper, tin and aluminium were established. Alberto is a true heir of this legacy as he is descended on his father's side from Giovanni and on his mother's, from Alfonso Bialetti of the octagonal cast aluminium coffee-maker fame. In 1924 the Alessi workshop produced trays and coffee pots under the name Fratelli Alessi Omegna (FAO) and four years later the company moved to Crusinallo where it is still located.

In the early 1930s, the eldest son of the founder, Carlo joined the company and designed the majority of its output throughout the decade, culminating in his 1945 masterpiece, the Bombé, which remains an Alessi bestseller today. Originally in nickel and silver with Bakelite handles, it came to define the company's brand identity and was symbolically, on the cover of *Paesaggio Casalingo*, a chronicle of the company's history by Alessandro Mendini. While it was in this period that

Alessi started research and testing on stainless steel as a material, it was only after the war and more so in the 1950s that it really took off and was used for mass production. Aside from this, the company under Carlo also experienced a turning point in its production process: it gradually switched from artisan work, using lathes and where the production depended on the craftsman who was also technician and artist, to industrial work using presses.

From the 1940s, Carlo retired from designing and turned to managing the company, which acquired a new trade name, Alfra (Alessi Fratelli) while his brother Ettore, who had joined the company in the 1945, developed Alessi's expertise in the cold-pressing of metals. According to Carlo in Patrizia Scarzella's *Steel & Style: The Story of Alessi Household Ware*, "The war period was a period of transition", and he meant it in terms of the production process, but on hindsight it also led to the company having an international aspect with high export rates, giving birth to the tradition of the Italian design factory that we know today.

A new figure was born, that of the designer, in the 1950s, with the first "designer" bar items of Luigi Massoni and Carlo Mazzeri. The decade also represented the end of chrome-and-silver-plated brass, and the adoption of stainless steel as primary material for the firm's output. Mazzeri also designed the expansion of the plant at Crusinallo, and in 1967 the trade name changed once again to Ceselleria Alessi. It was 1970 that represented yet another turning point for Alessi, with the coming onboard of Carlo's eldest son Alberto, fresh from his law degree at university. Initially concerned with commercial dealings and communicating new products, Alberto was in his early twenties, highly educated and brimming with ideas on design and its role in society. Confessing that "[…] yes, when I started working at Alessi in 1970, maybe I was a little too utopian […] The first projects I coordinated at that time clearly testify to that kind of approach." One of the most famous examples of this idealistic approach was the commissioning of Salvador Dali to create an "art multiple" together with some of the most interesting artists of that period. The final product defied everything the company had done up until then: not only could no one tell what it was for, it earned Alberto the disapproval of his uncle Ettore. Carlo stopped the project soon after.

Yet it was this gleeful, daring approach that Alberto never grew out of, and he has taken the company to greater heights than ever before with his willingness to run risks. Fiercely holding on to the belief that life has to be more than a banal matter of following the herd,

he declares that "as long as I have the breath of life […] I shall fight with all my might so that our lives might be filled with poetry." By the 1980s, he had become general manager and his brother Michele, manager of organisation and finance. The 1980s was also typified by the use of different metals. The new trade name Officina Alessi is indicative of this return to the workshop of the 1920s, but, as with Eliot's historical sense, it was with the knowledge of being "most acutely conscious of (its) place in time, of (its) contemporaneity". This means that even while the company was looking back, it was at the same time conscious of being in the midst of the Postmodern movement in architecture and design. The Tea and Coffee Piazza project which invited internationally-renowned architects to participate in designing tea and coffee services; the collaborations with the maestros, Achille Castiglioni, Michael Graves, Philippe Starck, Aldo Rossi and Mendini, demonstrated Alessi's historical sense that it was confident of being at the forefront of the Italian design factory phenomenon. The 1990s saw the beginning of their utilisation of plastic products with projects like Family Follows Fiction

under the research workshop-oriented Centro Studi Alessi. The participation of Stefano Giovannoni and Guido Venturini under King-Kong Productions was the clearest signal that Alessi was venturing into the playful, whimsical, sometimes ironic area of design. The Juicy Salif, Merdolino, Anna G., Graves family and Girotondo are all instantly recognisable icons amongst the output in this decade. In the first decade of the 21st century, two of the most noteworthy product lines are Giovannoni's Mr Chin and OrienTales, a tableware line in fruit and animal shapes resembling eye-catching toys. Yet Alessi has not abandoned its traditional material. The Tea and Coffee Towers in 2003, the younger sibling of the Tea and Coffee Piazza line in 1983, is a line of stunning services in mostly metal. It is a fitting symbol of Alessi today, and its historical sense of being inheritor of a rich heritage of design. On the one hand, it pays tribute to the presence of the past and its origins in the 1920s when Giovanni had his officina; on the other, it acknowledges its role as pre-eminent design factory in the brave new world of the 2000s where the new faces of architecture and design still remain to be crafted.

EVOLUTION OF THE ALESSI LOGO

1

1| The earliest incarnation of the Alessi logo. The origins of the Alessi company began in 1921, when Giovanni Alessi started producing different objects for the kitchen in brass and nickel silver in Italy's Strona Valley. FAO, which stands for Fratelli Alessi Omegna, or the Alessi Brothers Omegna, was used as the logo from 1921 to 1939.

2| With the end of FAO from 1945, the company was renamed as ALFRA, or ALessi FRAtelli, signifying the next generation of the Alessi brothers at the helm: Carlo Alessi and his younger brother, Ettore Alessi. This logo was designed by Carlo Alessi.

3| After Alberto Alessi joined Alessi in 1970, he decided to use only the Alessi surname in the logo. At this point, Alessi was starting to become part of a bigger group of Italian Design Factories and gaining international recognition. The designer Franco Sargiani helped Alberto Alessi to update the corporate image of the company. This logo by Sargiani was used from 1970.

ALESSI

OFFICINA
ALESSI

The latest Alessi logo, which is still being
used today, was designed by Studio
Sottsass Associati in the mid 1980s.
Since 2006, the logo is shared amongst
Alessi's three trademarks, Officina Alessi,
Alessi and A di Alessi.

THE PRODUCTS

THE HIT LIST.
PROJECTS.
COLLABORATIONS.
FIASCOS.

THE HIT LIST

Mendini's charismatic Anna G. cockscrew, Sottsass's glinting condiment set, Starck's alien-arachnid lemon squeezer. These iconic, almost totemic products are the very reflection of Alessi's excellence in design and craftsmanship. You may have seen these extraordinary metal architectures in Hollywood films, glossy magazines, even – and especially – the trendy homes of design aficionados.

While the ten products featured in The Hit List have tremendous design and emotional appeal, some are not as functional and practical when it comes to fulfilling their purpose as household ware. Take for famous example, Starck's Juicy Salif – the three-legged juicer apparently makes juicing more of a mess than a help and domestic use has been advised against, except as ornamental display. The question then remains: why are these products smash hits, as compared to other Alessi items? As Patrizia Scarzella comments on the 5070 Condiment Set in Steel & Style: The Story of Alessi Household Ware, *Sottsass' design "represents an emblematic case: it is an object with a specific purpose which owes its extraordinary commercial success not to its handiness but mostly to its look". The same applies to Starck's Juicy Salif – the three-legged juicer looks bizarre and yet, strangely, beautiful.*

The shortcomings of these extraordinary household items are almost completely irrelevant. In spite of their weaknesses, they remain the company's top bestsellers and highly coveted by consumers worldwide. The reason is simple: Alessi's iconic, edgy products never fail to make their presence felt on the domestic landscape with pieces that can put a smile on people's faces, a spring in their step, and a cheer in their hearts. There is always a guaranteed element of surprise in every product Alessi undertakes, which appeals to consumers not only aesthetically but also, more crucially, emotionally.

These beloved heroes in the Alessi repertoire remain at the top of their league for their ability, in Alberto's words, "to reach people's hearts, to always move on the enigmatic boundary line between what may become real (that is to say objects that are really loved and owned by people) and what will never become real (that is to say objects too far from what, at present, ordinary people are ready to wish and to use)." These bestsellers embody Alessi's design philosophy in practice by measuring the distance between dreams and reality and between emotion and function, and then bringing them just a little closer together.

BOMBÉ TEAPOT, CARLO ALESSI, 1945

To Alessandro Mendini, the Bombé represents "the symbol of the history of Alessi production." He points out several reasons for this. Socio-cultural ones include the iconic, recognisable form of the kettle and the identification of it being a product of Italian post-war culture. In a business sense, it incited a boost in Alessi's production and characterised the shift in Alessi's manufacturing concerns from craft (using lathes) to industrial ones (using presses).

The industrial processes throughout the years of the production of the Bombé include silver-plated brass, chrome-plated brass, stainless steel and Electro Plated Stainless Steel. The Bombé sports four sizes: the two, four, six and eight-cup versions; while the full set includes coffee pot, teapot, milk jug, sugar bowl and tray all quipped with bakelite handles.

As a second generation member of the Alessi management, Carlo joined Alessi in the 1930s; slowly but surely defining Alessi's style identity. Most Alessi products during this period were Carlo's, culminating in the Bombé, his final and most famous. It cemented his reputation as an important post-war industrial designer to watch, after his graduation from industrial design school in Novara in the early 1930s.

The curvy, elliptical shape was eye-catching and launched to popular acclaim, its form remaining in the collective imagination as quirky and dramatically blown-up. It also makes reference to several coffee pot designs throughout history which Alessi has manufactured under licence: an 1880 teapot by Christopher Dresser, Finnish architect Eliel Saarinen's Tea Set with Urn from 1933 and Marianne Brandt's Tea and Coffee Service from 1924.

In 1983, the Bombé tea and coffee set was reissued as part of the Antologia Alessi series, which took a critical retrospective look at iconic products with what is described in *Alessi The Design Factory*, a monograph on Alessi, as their "historical importance [...] design validity and [...] success with the public".

This iconic status was cemented with the publication of Mendini's *Paesaggio Casalingo*, a documentation of the company and its production history from 1921 to 1980. The Bombé was chosen as an emblem of such a history and was the sole product featured on the cover.

5070 CONDIMENT SET, ETTORE SOTTSASS, 1978

What Alberto Alessi calls Alessi's most archetypal product was almost not to be: the crystal manufacturer had deemed it impossible to produce due to the proposed method of securing the steel rods through a hole in the crystal. The company forged on and eventually launched it in 1978.

Today the 5070 Condiment Set, designed in collaboration with Sottsass' assistant Ulla Salovaara is Alessi's constant bestseller. Made from crystal glass and polished stainless steel, the set comes with four cruets and shakers for oil, salt and pepper, and a cellar for jams or parmesan cheese.

The legendary Italian industrial designer had Alberto Alessi star-struck when they first met in 1972. After all, this was the man who designed the iconic Olivetti Valentine and played a pivotal role in establishing Italy's prominence in the design field. Alberto recalls that "he was the first person of truly international standing with whom I had dealings [...] he was the first person I met through work who for me has become a real mentor, one of my maestros."

Fully bearing in mind dining rituals in Western cultural habits, Sottsass intended for the 5070 to store condiments, with all elements sitting in a stainless steel stand so that sauces, seasoning, spices or toothpicks could be passed round. Unostentatious and refined in its simplicity, the 5070 embodies the poetics of good design.

Citing the reasons for its continued success, Alberto names its pleasant form, good functional design and justified price, and imagines that there are no other oil cruets that can rival the 5070 in success.

Sottsass muses, "I think it is very hard to design a 'beautiful table': it does not depend simply on the tools and materials one uses, it depends on a subtle, fragile and uncertain sagacity."

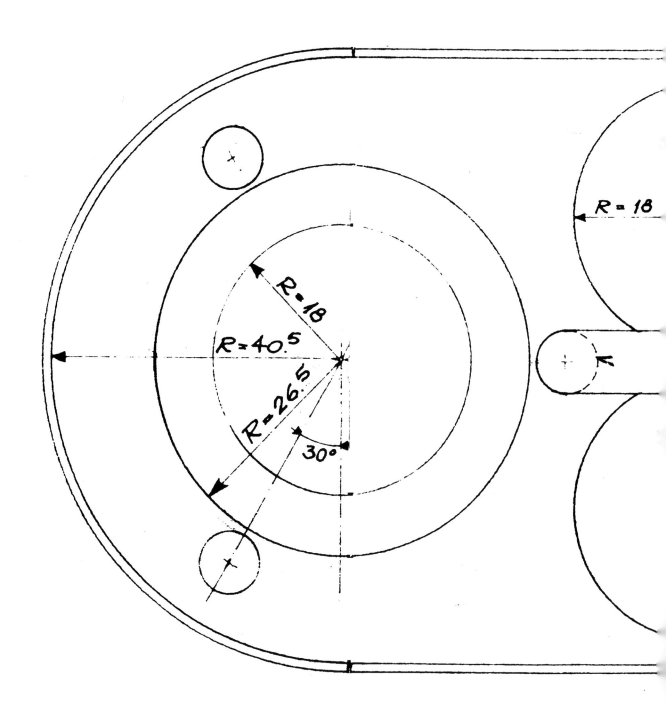

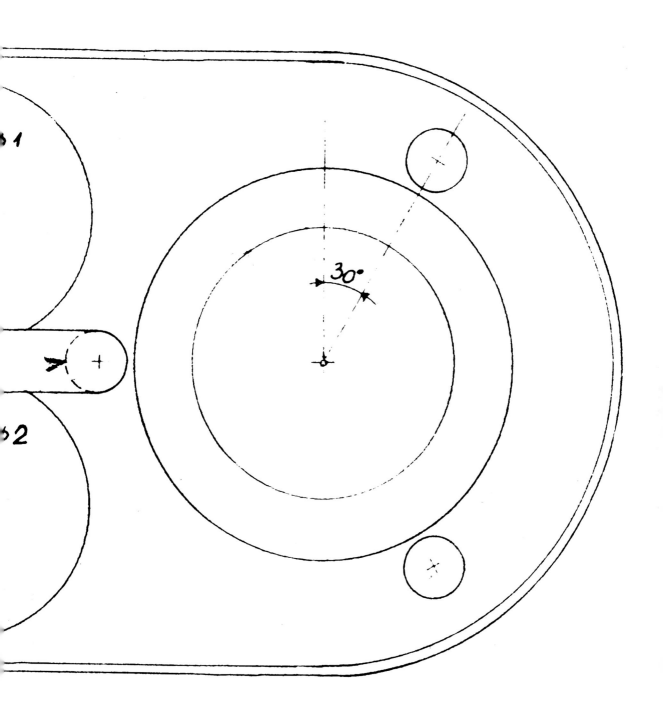

30°

LA CINTURA DI ORIONE, RICHARD SAPPER, 1979 ...

Identifying an invisible demographic and labelling them "home gourmets", Alessi defines them as "people who love creative gourmet cooking and who [...] will give themselves to the cooking play at home". Yet they are hampered by mass-produced stainless steel apparatus that fail to cater to more specialised needs.

La Cintura di Orione aimed to fill precisely that gap. Richard Sapper was commissioned to design a range of cooking utensils as an alternative to the convention of shaping all items in a range similarly, as well as the domination of stainless steel with aluminium thermo diffuser base.

Working together with Alberto Gozzi and some of the top practitioners of haute cuisine in Europe as consultants, Sapper created a line of equipment that was adapted to individual cooking methods and temperature considerations.

In order to make all the items in the range unique and different from each other, Sapper crafted all pots and pans from different metals, each suited as far as possible to the cooking method. Furthermore, there are actually three versions of the project. The 1986 original in thick copper lined with stainless steel is marketed under the premium Officina Alessi; while two other versions produced in the 2000s belong to the less pricey Alessi brand. Features include aluminium with a non-stick coating and a laminate of a layer of aluminium sandwiched between two layers of stainless steel.

Another example is the frying and crêpe pans, which are made of black iron heat regulation, and the oval cocotte for braising and stewing, which comes in cast iron to accommodate a steady, even flame. The shapes are also taken into consideration. Conical or cylindrical with flared or curved sides, they are moulded differently for specific types of cooking.

The big names involved as consultants and designers in collaboration with Sapper and Gozzi included Alain Chapel, Pierre and Michel Troisgros, Gualtiero Marchesi, Angelo Paracucchi, Roger Vergé, Jean-André Charial and Raymond Thuilier.

Part of Officina Alessi, the branch of the brand concerned with research and experiment, La Cintura di Orione was, from its inception, an ambitious project to produce "the most advanced line of cooking utensils ever mass produced". Today the line continues with new inventions like new trilaminate adaptations of older items that work on electromagnetic induction heating surfaces.

← Pots and pans in aluminium with non-stick coating, 2006.

→ Casserole with two handles in 18/10 stainless steel and copper, 1986.

overleaf Pots and pans in aluminium with non-stick coating, 2006.

previous spread   Image by Milton Glaser.

this page   Saucepan in aluminum with non-stick interior.
Handle in 18/10 stainless steel, 1988.

←   Stockpot in multiply, mirror polished, 2009.

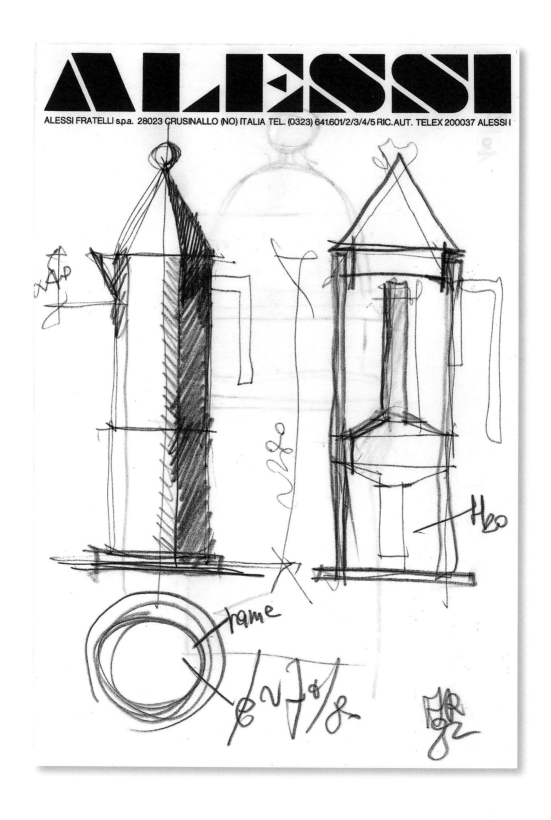

LA CONICA, ALDO ROSSI, 1984

Alberto Alessi has fond recollections of his late friend Aldo Rossi. Their early esteem for and rapport with each other resulted in the 1984 Alessi publication, The Conica, The Cupola and Other Cafetieres. *This was a collection of Rossi's designs for an affordable coffee maker for the masses.*

Some of these were put into production, most famously the La Cupola espresso maker, Il Conico kettle, the Ottagono espresso maker and the La Conica, the espresso maker so named for its lid. This last, besides being an Alessi bestseller since it was introduced, is a follow-up from Rossi's earlier collaboration with Alessi, the Tea and Coffee Piazza project. While elements of its form can be traced back to this earlier project, the La Conica was Rossi's first mass-produced design and an iconic product of the 1980s.

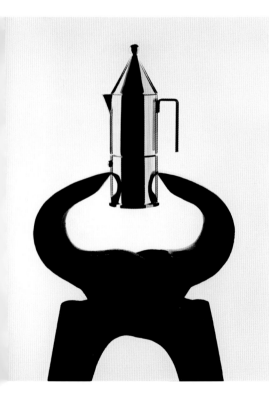

Specifically, it was one of the earliest designs that came under the Officina Alessi umbrella of products. Created just a year before the La Conica, Officina Alessi complemented the main Alessi range, aiming to execute designs based on research and experiments with form and methods of manufacture.

The La Conica is an exercise in stark, yet discreet geometry with its distinct, regular form, sharp, clean lines, and mirror-polished stainless steel finish. The conical straddles Rossi's interests in architecture and product design, embodying familiar archetypes in both fields.

The earliest steps in its manufacture were not that simple, however. Alberto's anecdotes recount Rossi presenting sketches and expecting the Alessi technical engineers to make changes and execute them. To then head of technical department and Giovanni's son Ettore Alessi's questions of bringing in more complete designs, Alberto recalls, "That was the only time I saw Rossi […] lose his temper, curtly answering that if he wanted some pretty technical designs he could get them from Zanuso and not from him."

Alessi understood then that most architects were more concerned about the strong ideas behind a design rather than technical specificities. "You know far better than me how to build a cafetiere," Rossi reportedly told Alessi's technical director, Casalino.

The strong ideas behind the La Conica are its simple, primary shape, its geometric precision and the negotiations between its architectural tropes and domestic functionality – ideas that guarantee its longevity in the Officina Alessi store of masterpieces.

"The cone, as everyone knows, is the name of a simple, solid geometric figure in the form of a round pyramid, produced by the rotation of a right triangle around one of its legs. This type of cone is known as "right" because its axis is perpendicular to the base." The analogy between the shape of the La Conica espresso coffee maker and its name is inescapable. La Conica owes its name to the lid.

La Conica, with its subtle, formal simplicity and its strong and familiar image, is a conceptual proposition of architectural archetypes and, at the same time, one of the most emblematic and best-loved items in contemporary product design.

GRAVES FAMILY, MICHAEL GRAVES, 1985 ...

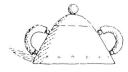 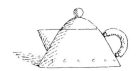

Calling a group of objects produced by a designer "a family" seems fitting for a company that is run by descendents of its founder. Graves himself expresses a mutual sentiment: "Perhaps most importantly, with Alessi, tradition extends to the idea of family. As a designer you and your people are brought in and treated as members of a family".

The Graves clan's patriarch is the 9093 kettle with the bird-shaped whistle and conical body, whose enormous commercial successes in America and Europe inspired further collaboration between Alessi and the architect already famous for his built works. The Graves Family is really an informal collection that comprises Graves' works for Alessi that are still in production. These include, among others, a milk jug and sugar bowl, a salt shaker, pepper grinder, a coffee cup and saucer.

The idea for the 9093 arose as a result of Alessi approaching Graves to design a tea kettle for the North American market. This came after the successful collaboration between them on the Tea and Coffee Piazza of 1983. Graves recalls that Alberto had told him "Americans need a kettle to boil water for their instant coffee". He had also advised him to avoid the problems of previous kettles such as the base not being large enough an area for water to boil quickly, and the handle being too near the flame when it was placed at the kettle's side.

The result was the 9093, with a broad base and handle extending over the top, but most famously for its bird-shaped whistle. Copied countless times, it almost overshadowed Graves' reputation as architect. Standing firmly as a design classic of the 1980s and 1990s, it also led to other products such as the milk jug and sugar bowl, with similar polished stainless steel and finished with light-blue handles of polyamide tube.

Regarding Alessi's success with Graves' products, Alberto points to his uncanny instinct at knowing what works with the public: "His gift is an incredible capacity to tune into public taste what appears to be a natural instinct." Significantly, Alessi has sold more units of the 9093 than any other product in its history.

→ Advertising image from Lowe Pirella, 2001.

Drawing by Lorenzo Mattotti

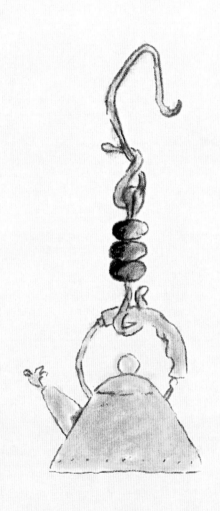

GIROTONDO, KING-KONG, STEFANO GIOVANNONI & GUIDO VENTURINI, 1989 ...

Named after an Italian nursery rhyme and featuring a motif of cut-out figures modelled after children's paper chains, the Girotondo series was underpinned by the principle of memory and emotional connection, specifically the connection everyone has to one's childhood. An explicit contrast to the design trends of the day dominated by the cerebral rigidity of 1980s design masters like Philippe Starck, the range under A di Alessi includes a wide variety of items from fruit bowls and containers to towels and jewellery.

Alberto explains the importance of the range to Alessi: "They were spot on with the 'playful style', they understood how important it is to work with 'emotional codes', but above all the project came at the right time, and its place in the Alessi catalogue hit the spot."

It was Alessandro Mendini who introduced the two young architects to Alberto in the late 1980s. With a suspicion that these were promising, emerging talents, Alberto gave them an introduction and a tour around the Alessi factory. The next time they met, Giovannoni and Venturini were armed with a book full of design notes.

According to the creators who had formed King-Kong Productions to research design and architecture, "The idea was to treat stainless steel as if it were paper, having the little men circling the edge as if they were holding hands and keeping together the objects in the bowl with their own 'girotondo'." Girotondo is the equivalent of the English nursery rhyme *Ring A Ring O' Roses*.

These eventually formed the basis for the Girotondo series of products under Family Follows Fiction, a research project that signalled the beginning of Alessi's foray into plastic and utilising of a playful, cartoon language to add to the existing domination of metal amongst the brand's products. The Girotondo range with its perforated figures come in both steel and plastic items.

Since its launch, the design of the little men has been copied substantially, becoming a recognisable icon that speaks to everyone's earliest memories.

1| *AKKO5*, fruit bowl
2| *AKKGT*, tray

ALL'ATTENZIONE DI GLORIA (DIR. TECNICA)
DA GIOVANNONI
GIROTONDO UFFICIO

PIANTA

TAGLIACARTE

PORTASCOTCH

APRIBUSTE
(ESTRUSO ALLUMINIO)
VEDI APRIBUSTA MHway

PORTABLOCCO
FOGLIETTI
10×10

PORTAMATITE/PORTABIGLIETTI

W
PORTABUSTE

PORTAGRAFFINI
TAGLIATO
↓ + BASSO

PORTABUSTE

U
SEZ

← MOLLETTA

LAMIERA
PIEGATA

PORTAMAT.
3

TAVOLETTA
PINZA
A4

PORTAMATITE 1

PORTAMATITE 2

JUICY SALIF, PHILIPPE STARCK, 1990

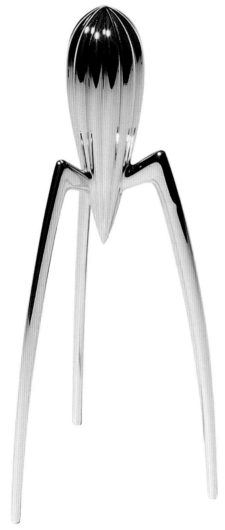

For Projet Solférino, a 1986 Alessi collaboration with design theorist and architecture critic Francois Burkhardt, Alberto Alessi had commissioned a stainless steel tray from product design maverick Philippe Starck. Starck responded with a 29-centimetre-tall hybrid of an alien and an arachnid that just happened to become one of the most significant design icons of the 20th century.

Other than winning a host of design prizes, being acquired for museums like the MOMA and making cameos in Hollywood movies, the lemon squeezer was the must-have designer product of young ambitious professionals in the 1990s. Alberto, in selecting it for Projet Solférino, appreciated that the product worked on a level of "figural creativity", expressing "sensorial values" that were independent of its function.

Alberto considers the cerebral and visceral aspects of the design, and identifies a sense of poetry that the Juicy Salif expressed and which spoke to so many people who own it. He considers that "a true work of design must move people, convey feelings, bring back memories, surprise, transgress [...] in sum, it has to be poetic. Design is one of the most apt poetic forms of expression of our day."

The cast alloy, three-legged utensil is also, famously, criticised as being impractical: apparently, the lemon juice squirts anywhere but the intended receptacle.

Alessi has been defiantly proud of the Juicy Salif in the face of such commentary. To celebrate the tenth anniversary of its launch, the brand has taken 10,000 and individually numbered and gold plated them. However, instructions indicate that these are for ornamentation only, as the citric acid from lemons would erode the gold plating.

The Juicy Salif has gone beyond being a functional kitchen tool into the realm of symbols that touch people emotionally. Speaking of the unusual design, its creator explains, "I very much like the idea of surprise, it is a sort of mental short circuit which can generate many other things and evoke a personal feeling for the user."

MERDOLINO, STEFANO GIOVANNONI, 1993

"The lavatory brush is made funny at last with the Merdolino. Toilet humour here takes the shape of a terracotta plant pot, in plastic of course, sprouting a curious green cactus," declares Alberto Alessi.

Humour, childlike playfulness and bright pops of colour abound in the Family Follows Fiction (FFF) workshop, part of the Centro Studio Alessi project, created to conduct research on design methodologies. Giovannoni's Merdolino toilet brush represents the interests of the workshop perfectly, in its colour, function and form. Employing the "cartoon effect" of a long succulent shrub growing from an elongated pot, the tool, which is rendered in colourful thermoplastic resin, resembles a child's toy accidentally left in the lavatory.

Giovannoni achieved instant notoriety for this product, Alessi's first bathroom item. He would later go on to design a whole bathroom, the Il Bagno Alessi One, but it was this humble toilet brush, what Alberto Alessi calls the "indispensable but taboo object", that became one of the most important objects under FFF.

When Merdolino was first introduced to the general public under the A di Alessi trademark, Giovannoni was criticised for his boldness in applying his design skills to such a vulgar product. But today, the Merdolino is firmly on Alessi's list of bestsellers and Giovannoni has been praised by Alberto as a designer par excellence. Alberto sees the toilet brush as "a welcome breath of poetry to which we were not used but which opened up whole new vistas in development".

Seeking to design products that would speak to the deepest, earliest desires of the adult, items in Family Follows Fiction have, according to Laura Polinoro, one of the founders of the Centro Studio Alessi, become "an instrument of play [...] tell(ing) short fables and [...] stimulating transposition into the fantastic." Most of these items are made from plastic, enhancing the toy-like feel and allowing for vivid hues, which serves to counter the familiar metals of the Alessi and Officina Alessi ranges.

ANNA G., ALESSANDRO MENDINI, 1994

scala 1 : 1

Alberto Alessi's admiration of her is noticeable in his glowing terms: "I'm especially proud of the Anna G. corkscrew, which immediately became our top bestseller, thereby debunking the rumour, slyly put about by the man himself, that Mendini only designs objects that don't sell!"

One of the Alessi products that truly deserves the cult status it has enjoyed since its inception, the Anna G. corkscrew went on to spawn a whole range of tableware produced from 1994 to 2001, from a cheese grater to a cigar lighter. Today it remains an Alessi bestseller, instantly recognisable as representative of the brand's design values.

Unveiling the design for a new Alessi corkscrew, Mendini presented to Alberto Alessi a woman with a magnetism and mysterious charisma that instantly captured hearts. Every element became part of a personality; Alberto pointed out the resemblance to one of Mendini's friends who had also designed for Alessi, the designer Anna Gili. With her bobbed hair, sharp features and slim figure, Anna G. had come to life.

Anna G. represented the face of Alessi that was fresh and modern with a sense of humour. Anna's head forms the handle while the body is a dress and the shoulders are the corkscrew's levers. Originally clad in red plastic (polyamide), and chrome-plated zamak, Anna G. wears dresses of myriad colours today.

The range has also expanded – Anna Cheese, a cheese grater; Anna Time, a timer; Anna Sparkling, a champagne cork; Anna Candle, a candlestick; Anna Stops 1 and 2, bottle stoppers; Anna Light, a cigar lighter and Anna Box.

Its endearing form has allowed for creative possibilities in advertising and styling. Anna G. has morphed into Marilyn Monroe and even inspired Mendini to design another corkscrew, the Sandro M., in the figure of a boy.

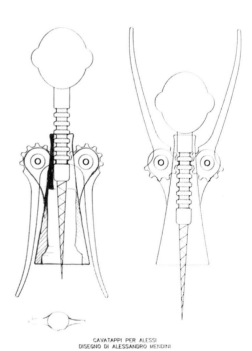

CAVATAPPI PER ALESSI
DISEGNO DI ALESSANDRO MENDINI

← Advertising image from Lowe Lintas Pirella Göttesche, 2000.

1| Anna G. figure outside a shop in Belgium.

2| Initially presented in 1994, the successful Anna G.
icon acquired cult status and generated a small family
of objects between 1994 and 2001.

3| The Alessandro M. Band. A project by
Alessandro Mendini and Massimo Caiazzo.
Photography by Riccardo Bianchi.

→ Exhibition image for Il Bagno Alessi dOt by Christoph Radl.

1| *Banana Kid*, sugar bowl, 2008
2| *Lily Pond*, *Lotus* and *Lily Bird*, sushi set, small bowl and soy sauce container, 2008
3| *Fruit Sugar Bowl*, sugar bowl, 2008

ORIENTALES, STEFANO GIOVANNONI, 2007 …

2

3

A national museum specialising in Chinese artefacts approaches an Italian company that prides itself on being a "research laboratory in the applied arts" in the finest tradition of Italian design. Several product ranges resulted, all inspired by Oriental motifs. This partnership between Alessi and Taiwan's National Palace Museum began in 2007, with the Taiwanese government's desire to promote Chinese culture on a global scale. Stefano Giovannoni was commissioned to design the mascot.

While The Chin Family products were human figurines clad in traditional Chinese costumes and rendered in thermoplastic resin, OrienTales extends the ideas in a wider range of materials. Here, melamine and ceramic sushi sets are lily ponds, fine bone china milk jugs morph into paradise birds and egg cups become goldfish.

Like the Louvre, Taiwan's National Palace Museum has witnessed a long and tumultuous history. Since its last expansion, the museum has completed its inventory of collections; the collaboration with Alessi and Giovannoni is part of the move to establish itself as a global museum of the 21st century. Tellingly, the Alessi book on the range is subtitled *Eastern Stories through Western Eyes.*

Launched as part of A di Alessi, OrienTales exemplifies the witty contemporary design and reasonable prices that the range was created for. The effect of a toy set or fairy tale is unmistakable, and is testament to Giovannoni's approach to design, which is playful, energetic and innovative, as well as his unique interpretation of the artistic lineage of the Far East.

Yet with every individually hand-decorated piece of the collection, what is evident is the attention paid to craft and quality, something Alberto defines as "a kind of handicraft made with the help of machines".

Fittingly, the intricate, colourful and almost fantastical monkeys, fish and birds resemble ancient Chinese porcelain trinkets and are a nod to Asian craft traditions; even the cutlery set is designed for the Oriental table – chopsticks, chopstick holders and tiny dishes for soy sauce.

Lotus, small bowl, 2008

Banana Bros, salt and pepper set, 2009

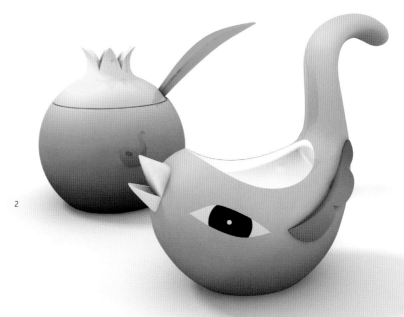

1| *Paradise Birds*, salt and pepper set, 2008
2| *Paradise Bird* and *Fruit Sugar Bowl*, milk jug and sugar bowl, 2008
3| *Lily Pond*, *Lotus* and *Lily Bird*, sushi set, small bowl and soy sauce container, 2008
4| *Banana Boys*, set of three caps, 2009
5| *Banana Bros*, salt and pepper set, 2009

3

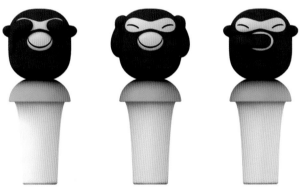

4

5

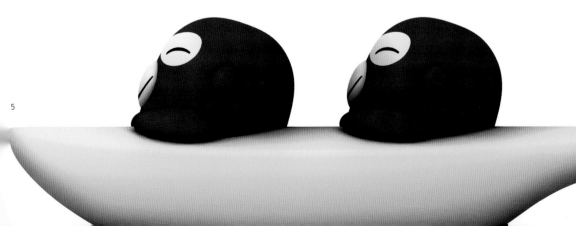

Banana Family, 2009. left ▶ right: *Banana Charm*, cell phone charm | *Banana Split*, hand-decorated bookmarker in thermoplastic resin |
Sweet Banana, sugar castor | *Banana King*, salt, pepper and spice grinder | *Banana Queen*, salt, pepper and spice grinder |
Josephine Banana, kitchen timer | *Banana Mon-Key*, key ring

SPECIAL PROJECTS

Alessi considers their items to embody values other than being useful. In today's society and modern life, people desire objects that speak to them emotionally. "By choosing those items that will become part of their personal environment," says Alberto Alessi, "they bestow on them important social significance, using them as motifs to communicate values they consider to be part of themselves." For that very purpose, Alessi has devoted two special projects that reflect a deeper meaning with possession of their products.

The first collection of miniatures was thus created. Comprising Alessi's most recognisable designs produced in the last 60 years – Mendini's 100% Make Up and Anna G., Rossi's La Conica, Graves' 9093 kettle, Gehry's Pito, Starck's Dédé, Hot Bertaa and Juicy Salif, King Kong's Girotondo, Carlo Alessi's Bombé teapot as well as Giovannoni's Mami, this delicate collection, the first of a planned line of similar sets, is dedicated to Alessi's devoted collectors with special consideration of space and cost. As a scaled-down replica, the miniatures only measure one-third of the original design's size. Despite a significant shrink in size, these lithe objets d'art, perfectly reproduced with every detail intact, preserve the exquisite appearance and craftsmanship of Alessi's classics.

Other than impulse, sentiment or personal desire, there is another reason why people buy things: for a good cause. With T-DREAM and Mendini's Alessandro M. – Sun Dream, Alessi channels their design expertise into products that can make a difference to those less fortunate. In support of the International Amici dei Bambini association, the Italian design factory launched T-DREAM in 2007, a collection of T-shirts designed by eight internationally renowned designers, and Alessandro M. – Sun Dream, a corkscrew resembling a boy with the same name as their creator, in 2008. All these are part of The Dream Factory project that Alessi and Amici dei Bambini developed, "with the aim of making the dreams of orphan children all over the world a reality," states Alberto. The proceeds from the sale of these designer items will be donated to help realise the dreams of many underprivileged children in orphanages in Brazil and Mongolia, especially those that are considered too old for adoption and too young to enter society.

ALESSI MINIATURES

Own a design classic at a fraction of the price: the Alessi Miniatures, Alessi's first collection of their all-time premium bestsellers wrought small, does just that. These icons culled from the finest in the vast range of smash hits over the last sixty years of production were reproduced at one-third the size of the originals. The toy-like scale – the tallest in the range measures a lofty 128 millimetres – shows off the elegant, intricate craftsmanship that these items have been loved for all over the world. Created with collectors in mind, these diminutive treasures include Carlo Alessi's Bombé teapot from 1945, Aldo Rossi's La Conica from 1984 and Stefano Giovannoni's Mami from 1999.

100% Make Up, Alessandro Mendini, 42 × 128 mm

La conica, Aldo Rossi, 40 × 26 × 80 mm

9093, Michael Graves, 73 × 78 mm

Pito, Frank Gehry, 70 × 60 × 76 mm

Anna G., Alessandro Mendini, 30 × 100 mm

Hot Bertaa, Philippe Starck, 105 × 60 × 83 mm

Girotondo, King-Kong, 77 × 40 mm

Bombé, Carlo Alessi, 72 × 44 × 50 mm

Mami, Stefano Giovannoni, 98 × 75 × 74 mm

Juicy Salif, Philippe Starck, 40 × 45 × 115 mm

Citrus basket, Ufficio Tecnico Alessi, 75 x 75 mm

Cocktail shaker, Luigi Massoni, Carlo Mazzeri, 30 x 65 mm

5070 condiment set, Ettore Sottsass, 60 x 25 x 60 mm

9090 espresso coffee maker, Richard Sapper, 40 x 70 mm

9091 kettle, Richard Sapper, 80 x 55 x 70 mm

Girotondo, King-Kong, 135 mm

Fruit Mama, Stefano Giovannoni, 110 × 90 mm

Firebird, Guido Venturini, 40 × 20 × 105 mm

La Cubica, Aldo Rossi, 55 × 75 × 65 mm

9093, Michael Graves, 73 × 78 mm

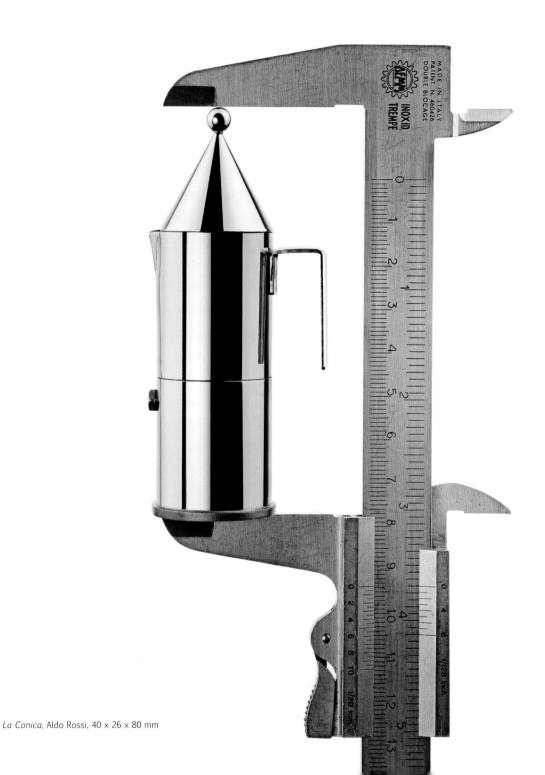

La Conica, Aldo Rossi, 40 × 26 × 80 mm

T-DREAM & ALESSANDRO M. – SUN DREAM

T-DREAM & ALESSANDRO M. – SUN DREAM

1| *T-DREAM* by Aldo Rossi
2| *T-DREAM* by Alessandro Mendini
3| *T-DREAM* by Stefano Giovannoni
4| *T-DREAM* by Riccardo Dalisi

1| *T-DREAM* by Martí Guixé
2| *T-DREAM* by Michael Graves
3| *T-DREAM* by Robert Venturi
4| *T-DREAM* by Philippe Starck

T-DREAM & ALESSANDRO M. – SUN DREAM

T-DREAM and Alessandro M. – Sun Dream were projects launched in 2007 and 2008 respectively, with a series of limited-edition products that were sold for the A di Alessi cause. For T-DREAM, eight famous international designers came together to design a collection of T-shirts, the profits of which would fund Amici dei Bambini's projects in Nepal, Colombia and Peru. Mendini's Alessandro M. – Sun Dream emerged a year later, and all proceeds from the sale of these products are donated to help the underprivileged children in orphanages in Brazil and Mongolia.

Alessandro M. wears an adorable sky-blue costume covered in fluffy white clouds, a costume that signifies hopes and dreams for children who do not have the luxury of indulging their dreams. Designed by Mendini in the likeness of his famous corkscrew, Alessandro M. – Sun Dream is part of the charity project by A di Alessi in collaboration with the international Amici dei Bambini association which Alessi has supported for many years. The charity is an international humanitarian aid organisation for the protection of children's right to have a family, and has helped many children and youths reintegrate into society for over 20 years through international cooperation and adoption. Being a "research lab in the applied arts", Alessi has always been in the creative business of transforming dreams and desire into tangible objects. With the same mission

of bringing "a little more happiness to all people" as Alberto has declared, A di Alessi pledged to help abandoned children in orphanages around the world realise their dreams.

Adoption and the possibility of finding a place within a new family is a possibility that blesses very few children otherwise confined to orphanage life. Especially for minors between the ages 11 to 18, the prospect of adoption is almost close to none. "Those who stand in benefit of this initiative are children who are living in a sort of 'limbo'", shares Marco Griffini, Chairman of Amici dei Bambini, "who too early in life have lost all hopes of becoming sons and daughters, and simply aren't ready to enter the adult world, all alone". Alessi joins Amici dei Bambini in "adopting" the dreams of these abandoned youths by helping to develop a life project that will allow them, one day, to enjoy a stable job, their own family and a better future.

Starting from 2009 the partnership between Alessi and Amici dei Bambini will take a step forward: the "dream factory" will go back to the children whose dreams have already been realised, all around the world, and help them to develop an individual project in a long-term perspective, aiming to realise the biggest dream of all: to leave the orphanage, one day, and be able to have a better life outside.

EXTERNAL COLLABO-RATIONS

In an interview with Indianapolis Monthly, Alberto discloses the naughty design proposal that his brothers did not want to produce: a vibrator named "Joystick". The other collaborations with external companies, brands or designers seem tame by comparison. Yet Alessi has consistently managed to inject a dose of their radical creativity into products, ranging from cars and telephones to textiles and stickers, that do not fit right into the traditional Alessi catalogue.

The mismatched marriages between Alessi and other external companies may be rather surprising, but in essence, the strange bedfellows are unique collaborations that correspond to Alessi's design philosophy in manifesting art and poetry into tangible objects. "The new and successful products of the near future must be able to ply the imagination of the general public," states Alberto Alessi. "They must have a powerful epiphanic impulse. They must be irresistible, and this can only be achieved if they are able to open the doors to the immensity of creative potential."

And the kitchen is not the only place where designs can expand that creative potential and imaginations. "Cars, refrigerators, televisions and the like are becoming more standardised," observes Alberto. Despite not having manufactured these industrial products previously, Alessi is constantly its pushing its boundaries by merging its strengths with the skills of other companies to transform the ordinary into extraordinary.

The collaborative efforts with external companies have proven to be fruitful. With automobile giant Fiat, Alessi created Fiat Panda Alessi, an innovative concept car with a refreshing interior that makes heavy city traffic less agonising. In addition to the number of timekeeping pieces in Alessi's catalogue, Alessi and Seiko jointly produced a series of watches that not only conveys the time, but also class and style. Together with international bathroom companies Laufen and Oras, two bathroom lines by Stefano Giovannoni and Wiel Arets were launched. Also, for a world-renowned kitchenware maker, the progression to sinks, hobs, hoods and faucets was a natural one, resulting in La Cucina Alessi, a complete Alessi kitchen made in partnership with Valencina and Oras, that evoked domestic food rituals.

The list goes on. As part of the evolution of Alessi, a myriad new products have increasingly made their way into the company's expanding catalogue – products such as pens, phones, tiles, barbeque pits, stickers and textiles. All these projects would not be possible without Alessi's willingness to make the leap in favour of ambitious and radical experiments, in support of companies that share the same spirit, audacity and sheer bravura.

FIAT
PANDA
ALESSI

Image by Christoph Radl

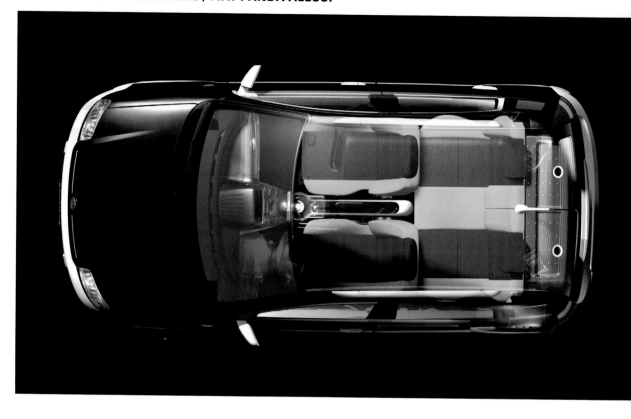

Trust an Italian design factory to bring a dash of creative wit, canny astuteness and aesthetic allure into the volatile arena of industrial design – even if it means venturing outside its own specialty. Indeed, Alessi has stretched its expertise beyond the fine heritage of designer kitchenware and gone ahead to develop new areas of product design they have never embarked on. For a brand renowned for its radical design experiments, Alessi has joined hands with designers and architects from other companies, providing playgrounds for them to develop their artistic and poetic imaginations on different sorts of machines. These creative adventures with their partners-in-crime saw Alessi conquering the product territories of watches, bathroom and cars, just to name a few.

"One of my greatest dreams," says Alberto Alessi, "has been to demonstrate the contribution that the practice of an Italian design factory like Alessi can make towards expanding our horizons." By forging partnerships with other renowned companies, Alessi has taken steps to make that dream a reality. In 2004, the unexpected collaboration between Alessi and Fiat gave birth to the Fiat Panda Alessi, an innovative concept car that outshines any generic mass-produced vehicle on the road. Stefano Giovannoni, the Italian architect and industrial designer famed for the Girotondo line, was the man behind the Fiat Panda Alessi project.

Approaching car design for the first time, Giovannoni nevertheless worked some gleaming design magic on the Fiat Panda. The objective of this project was to redesign one of the Italian automobile maker's recent models instead of producing a design blueprint for a completely new car. Preserving the exterior form, the interior of the car was given a new lease of life by the use of colours and masking. "I tried to perform a restyling that essentially maintained the design of the basic vehicle, yet giving it a young, fresh, extroverted and colourful image," says Giovannoni. Named Car of the Year 2004, the Fiat Panda is the exemplar of a brilliant masterpiece that resulted from a stylistic dialogue between two industries striving similarly for design excellence.

While Alberto continues to dream of an Alessimobile – a "trick" of a toy car made of painted tin he wanted Philippe Starck to work on and present to automobile manufacturers – other external collaborations involve designing objects with other types of wheels and gears. Alessi Watches is one such project. Adding to the stable of timepieces manufactured by Alessi, the company has also developed a range of watches with Seiko Instruments Inc. of Tokyo, Japan.

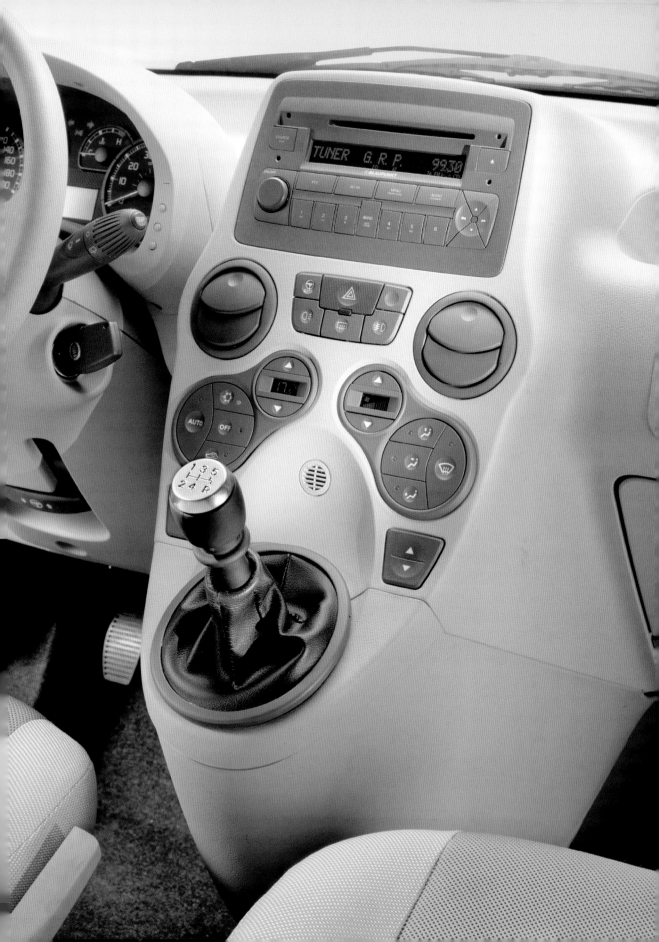

ALESSI
WATCHES

Tanto x Cambiare, Franco Sargiani with Stefano Roversi, 2008

Tanto x Cambiare, Franco Sargiani with Stefano Roversi, 2008

1

2

3

4

5

6

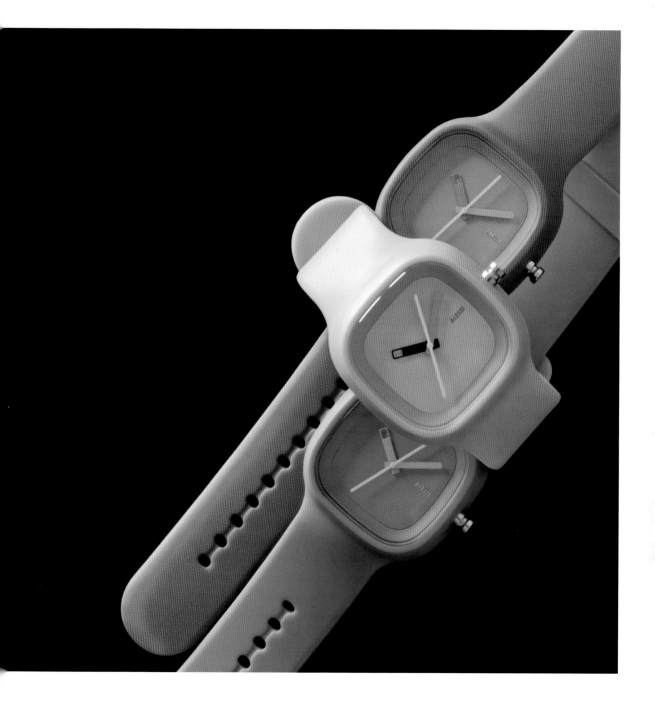

1| top ▶ bottom: *Ray*, Stefano Giovannoni, 2009 | *Arc*, Hani Rashid, 2007 | *Mariposa*, Miriam Mirri, 2007 |
Tanto x Cambiare, Franco Sargiani with Stefano Roversi, 2008 | *Millennium*, Miriam Mirri, 2008 |
Ciclo, Ettore Sottsass, 2006 | *Daytimer*, Will Alsop with Federico Grazzini, 2009. Image by Christoph Radl.
2| *Millennium Jr.*, Miriam Mirri, 2008. Rendering by Frederic Gooris.
3| *Calumet*, Stefano Pirovano, 2002.
4| *Tanto x Cambiare*, Franco Sargiani with Stefano Roversi, 2008.
5| *Millennium Jr.*, Miriam Mirri, 2008. Rendering by Frederic Gooris.
6| *Callisto*, Stefano Pirovano, 2002. Photography by Santi Caleca.
7| *Kaj*, Karim Rashid, 2005. Photography by Santi Caleca.

IL
BAGNO
ALESSI

Il Bagno Alessi One

Together, Alessi and Seiko created a new Alessi line of watches, with the first collection consisting of designs by Aldo Rossi, Achille Castiglioni, Richard Sapper, Matteo Thun and Mario Botta, all produced in the late 1980s. To date, the successful collaboration between the two companies has produced 19 different models of watches of watches designed by names well known for collaborating with Alessi. "Both jewellery and a business card", as Richard Sapper has noted, each exciting collection of watches reflects the designer's eccentricity and style, matched with the very best in state-of-the-art techniques in watch-making.

Designing cars and watches may not have coincided with Alessi's expertise in kitchenware, but there are some new territories that remain close to home. In conjunction with Swiss company Laufen and Oras from Finland, Il Bagno Alessi is an excellent example of Alessi's ability to channel its creativity and build extraordinary environments for the home, in this case the bathroom. "Not many objects for the bathroom, in fact, be they large or small, have really interesting, amusing, poetic design", shares Alberto. "Il Bagno Alessi takes this fact as its starting point and seeks to fill this gap."

Beginning with Il Bagno Alessi One by Giovannoni, the bathroom became another domestic landscape where Alessi explores more artistic possibilities. Sanitary ware,

bath tubs, shower cabins, furniture and accessories were given a fresh new make-up, provoking different perspectives on what seems to be a personal and private space. Following the success of Il Bagno Alessi One, Alessi launched Il Bagno Alessi dOt, a second bathroom project by contemporary Dutch architect Wiel Arets.

Alberto describes Arets, a designer from Alessi's Tea & Coffee Towers project: "From the instant I received his earliest sketches I began thinking that this peculiar Dutch architect, at once both pragmatic and intensely intellectual, could become one of our 'design heroes' of the 2000s." For Il Bagno Alessi dOt, Arets invigorated the bathroom scene in a formal and minimalist style, also taking into account the importance of bathroom organisation. Revolving around the fluidity of water, Arets' project pays attention to even the minutest details from the taps to the fittings.

External collaborations have, as Alberto as pointed out, "been a journey where real progress has always been looked for by exploring that territory which is situated between the Possible and the Real, between the area of the day and the area of the night." Alessi's cars, watches and bathrooms inhabit that moment of enchantment when night and day cross paths – just as dawn breaks, the first light of day appears, and a world of possibilities awaits.

DESIGN FIASCOS: THE ALESSI DREAM OF POSSIBILITY

Watching a beloved product sink or swim on its own merit in the choppy waters of the market is part of being an Italian design factory. Alessi goes further: embracing design fiascos, or products which fail to achieve commercial success, Alessi regards each design fiasco as a precious opportunity to perceive the "borderline" which separates the "area of the possible" from the "area of not possible". The "area of the possible" represents products easily understood and accepted by the consumer market; the "area of the not possible" represents projects too difficult to be understood and accepted by customers.

Unlike most mass production companies which stick to the well-beaten path with products safe, predictable and increasingly homogenous, Alessi is undaunted by risky projects, pursuing them with sensibility, intuition and courage. "My practice as an Italian design factory is different; our destiny is exactly the one to live as close as possible to the borderline," shares Alberto Alessi, "It means that we accept to play exactly on the borderline between the possible and not possible."

While the commercial success of a product would rarely reveal this "borderline", it is through Alessi's spirit of curiosity and adventure, resulting in a proud history of design fiascos, that they have discovered where this line resides.

Creative failures have watered the fertile soil of invention at Alessi, providing a valuable and accurate reflection on what people want beyond the capabilities of any marketing research tool. "I cannot tell you how exciting it may be to develop a new project knowing that it is straight on the borderline, but still on the right side of it," Alberto lets on. A design of such fortunate birth would most likely be both a commercial hit and at the same time, offer what Alessi regards as the "correct" contribution by an industrial company to today's consumer society, which is to push the boundaries of creativity and design in products.

Such is Alessi's belief in the philosophy of dancing on the borderline that the company becomes concerned if a fiasco does not take place that year – it would mean Alessi was losing its leading position in design excellence. This chapter tells the stories of five design fiascos – Hot Bertaa by Philippe Starck, Phil by Archille Castiglioni, The Soundtrack by Ron Arad, Mama-ò by Andrea Branzi, and Strelka by Marc Newson – and discusses the ways that each project skirts the category of commercial success despite the wealth of possibility that its design creates.

HOT BERTAA,
—*Philippe Starck.*
[mistake: function]

The Hot Bertaa will go down in history as "the (in)famous not-working kettle" by Philippe Starck. In production for seven years in the 1990s, the Hot Bertaa was discontinued in 1997 because it was functionally too complicated, failing to efficiently perform the assumed functions of a kettle.

During the design stage, the Hot Bertaa's compact, almost sacred appearance was shrouded with an aura of mysticism. The original design was to contain an inscription in Latin on the base. Starck wanted to create a masterly, sculptural object which would reflect his theory of "immovable aerodynamics" – to give a static object a feeling of movement. The aluminum Hot Bertaa kettle is shaped in the oblique style of Howitzer, pierced by a thermo plastic conical tube which functions on one end as a handle and the other as a spout, where water would be poured out.

The project took five long years of development, and baffled engineers on how to develop the mechanisms to ensure the steam and water would "exit" where they were intended. In order to fill the kettle, water would be poured in through the "handle". The steam produced during boiling would exit through the same handle, making the kettle potentially dangerous to use. For the end-user, using the Hot Bertaa required, perhaps, a little too much effort. In the words of Alberto Alessi, "You shouldn't need an instruction manual to operate a kettle"

The Hot Bertaa would eventually find its place in Alessi's design history, despite Starck's opinion that the Hot Bertaa was his "worst project ever". The minimalist and sculptural qualities of the kettle made it appear akin to a religious object. "Actually, the technical thinking behind the Hot Bertaa is deep and well-made," remarks Alberto on the mechanism of a ball bearing inside the kettle which prevents steam from escaping when water is being poured. Despite the kettle's impracticality, Alessi considers the Hot Bertaa one of Starck's great successes for Alessi, a design not solely justified by technology or commercial success, but a design which conveys Starck's ability to move people and to convey emotion.

PHIL
—Achille
Castiglioni
[Mistake: pricing]

The marketing brief for a new oil and vinegar set was especially challenging for Achille Castiglioni in 1982: to design an oil and vinegar set matching the success of Ettore Sottasass' 5070 set released in 1978, but at half the retail price. Following an intense period of research on the use of stainless steel wire, Castiglioni's final design for the condiment set was imbued with a feeling of great lightness in the stainless steel wire handle. "Unfortunately, the perceived value of the wire was not good enough, even if related to the low price point," remarks Alberto Alessi. Ironically, the Phil project helped propel the popularity and success of Sottsass' 5070 (Sottsass was known to periodically thank Castiglioni for his help). The company took around ten years to sell all the Phil cruets which were produced in high volumes.

While the Phil cruets did not enjoy great commercial success, it is regarded by Alessi as an extremely important project, a testimony to Castiglioni's "spark", his passion to pursue innovative ideas with a high degree of interest in the themes he deals with.

THE SOUNDTRACK
—*Ron Arad*
[mistake: communication]

"The Soundtrack is one of the most brilliant projects I have come across in at least ten years," writes Alberto Alessi following the release of Ron Arad's The Soundtrack CD rack in 1998. A self-adhesive CD storage system made from thermoplastic resin, The Soundtrack is simple and easy to use. Made with a minimum amount of material, it is considered to be more of a gift than an object. The Soundtrack is a concrete example of what Alessi calls "less is more", a personification of "immaterial design" of the 21st century, without the presence of the authoritative personal style of the designer. "I consider this fiasco not a good test of the intelligence of the customers", remarks Alberto.

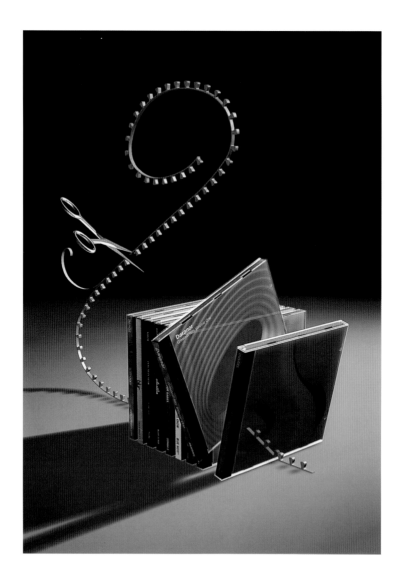

MAMA-Ò
—Andrea Branzi
[mistake: communication and sensoriality-memory-imagination]

Part of Officina Alessi, the 18/10 stainless steel Mama-ò kettle by Andrea Brazi was designed in 1988 and went into production in 1992. Possessing a whistle, the Mama-ò produces a melodic sound when the water boils and steam escapes from the caps.

While the Mama-ò was priced similarly to Michael Graves' kettle and was free of the functional woes of the Philippe Starck's Hot Bertaa, the presence of two symmetrical spouts instead of one in the kettle proved to be a source of bewilderment. "People were confused about which spout to use and so passed on to the following kettle on the shelf," remarks Alberto Alessi. Measured against two of Alessi's formal assessment criteria for its products, the Mama-ò revealed the borderline on two accounts: communication (customers were unable to understand how to use the Mama-ò) and sensoriality, memory and imagination (rather than pleasing the senses, the design of the Mama-ò became disorienting for the customer).

STRELKA
—Marc Newson
[mistake: pricing]

Alessi calls Australian industrial designer Marc Newson's Strelka cutlery set "an extraordinary event in the history of flatware". At the level of industrial production, the Strelka cutlery collection challenged production capabilities, due to the handle of each piece which possessed an asymmetrical double wall in stainless steel.

Hailed as a technical and production feat, the Strelka cutlery set expressed Newson's well-known sculptural style. The touch and manipulation of the Strelka cutlery was unlike any other cutlery set in the market when it was released in 2003. When gripped, each knife, fork and spoon gave a new and balanced feeling in one's hand. Alessi regards the Strelka collection as Newson's best project for Alessi. However, the Strelka is also, not surpisingly, the most expensive range of cutlery produced by Alessi. Alessi once again danced on the borderline: the very high price of the Strelka cutlery set was not accepted by the customer.

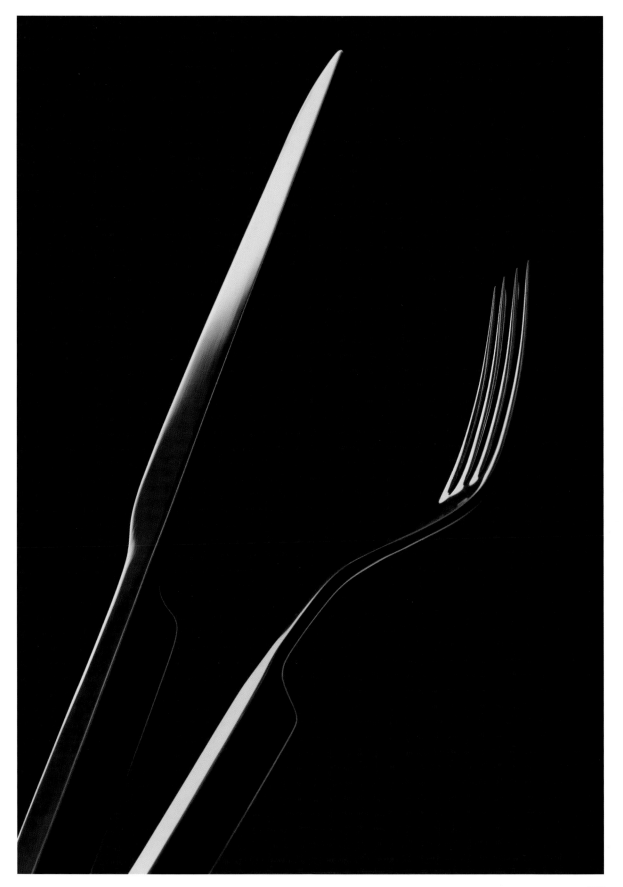

DREAMING OUT LOUD

Fools rush in where angels fear to tread. If so, then Stefano Giovannoni must be the trickster with his playful Girotondo cut-out manikins and mischievous monkeys, Michael Graves the stand-up comedian making people smile with colourful birds perched on kettle spouts and Philippe Starck the wisecracking life of the party with his peculiar contraptions. Alessandro Mendini has admitted he is the "joker in the pack". And Alberto Alessi? The jester behind it all in his own court.

These fools should be celebrated if the angels of "mass production and big industry", as Alberto identifies in 'New Notes on Alessi Practice', are the ones fearing to break established boundaries and tread on unknown territory, "(f)or they have led to a world of products so stale, drab and copied from each other that in my opinion the public, having no further reason to desire them, will soon refuse to buy them at all." One of the most popular industrial designers today, the Dutchman Marcel Wanders, expresses a similar ethos: "It is our responsibility to be magicians, to be jesters, to be alchemists." Alberto would agree; one of the tasks of the designer is to inject that bit of wonder, sprinkle that bit of stardust over everyday life where "stale, drab and copied from each other" products crowd. In other words, to conjure up a reality where objects speak to people's desire, to jest seriously and revel in the oxymoron, and to be the alchemist turning metals to gold – a not unsuitable metaphor for Alessi.

Alessi under Alberto's leadership has evolved to be one of the boldest, most fearless risk-takers in the design industry. It is testament to Alberto's courage to dream and to take inventive risks that Alessi is today recognised as foremost when it comes to the tradition of Italian design factories. When it comes to new products, he ascribes one of the tenets of his success formula to what he terms the "parameter of Sensoriality-Memory-Imagination. Its purpose is to gauge the sensorial pleasure and the grip on the public's imagination". This is the man who decides on which products to manufacture based on memory and the imagination, the same man who, in 1971, just after he joined the company under his father and uncle, commissioned Salvador Dali to produce an item which function, until today, no one can identify. Alberto himself has admitted it was one of his first "fiascos". It was to be the first of many over the next decades, and the following sections showcase some of these, together with unreleased prototypes as well as experimental projects the company has embarked on. Wise men say, only fools rush in. Alberto has proved to be the wisest of all and it is he who gets the last laugh after all.

FAMILY
FOLLOWS
FICTION

Family Follows Fiction (FFF) was launched in 1991 as one of two inaugural operations – or metaprojects – under the Centro Studi Alessi (CSA), a research initiative to investigate experimental new methodologies in the design field together with young designers. Exploring disciplines from communication and anthropology to art and marketing, FFF started with the motivation to arrive at fresh insights for the company. Specifically, the CSA works first by conducting research on the theoretical concept of the potential metaproject. Next comes the defining stage, where the metaproject identifies and delineates specific criteria, directions, as well as select the designers to be involved. Then, the designers and the technical team meet at workshops, producing first drafts and shortlisting the group of projects that will undergo further development. FFF was conceived and given birth to by such a process, under the direction of Alberto's project consultant Laura Polinoro. The other metaproject was Memory Containers, which considered the ritualistic aspects of serving food.

Yet, on hindsight, it was arguably FFF in the 1990s, and Alessi's venturing into plastic as a new material during the same period, that opened new doors in terms of colour, design and production processes. FFF showed the world a new face of the company that until then dealt primarily in steel and various metals. It was the driving force in the direction of Alessi's identity in the 1990s, an impact which continues to be felt today. Alberto formulates his intentions for the company in *New Notes on Alessi Practice*:

Prompted by a number of consultants as well as by our own curiosity, we felt the urgent need for an operation that would balance the authoritativeness, expressive impact and culturalisation of the projects developed for us by the "great masters" in the 1980s. This would be done by introducing a more emphatic, affective and confidential note into our catalogue [...] My intention, therefore, was to explore more explicitly and directly a number of expressive keys, such as play, memory and emotive involvement that were certainly already present, though in a more hidden form, in the works of those designers.

What he is pointing at is the need for a bold, stimulating experience that would appeal in new ways to our senses, and it was beginning to seem that the cerebral designs of the über-designers of the 1980s who have designed for Alessi – the likes of which included Michael Graves, Aldo Rossi and Robert Venturi – did not, according to Polinoro, speak to "our most delicate, tender, intimate and affective" selves.

Objects, Alessi believes, act. They behave in ways that have an affective impact, a quality that is sentimental, passionate and that deals at a gut level, bypassing judgement and mental evaluation. Working at the level of desire, ardour, sympathy and joy, some objects have the ability to trigger the most cherished feelings that lie closest to our hearts. This trigger is believed to be the element of play, the activity that does not achieve an apparent pragmatic purpose, which has to be indulged in, the secret pleasure by which people define themselves in private. What Alessi terms the "object-toy" was a way to answer the question: "In a room full of objects a child chooses one to relieve his boredom and solitude; why that object in particular?" The power held within an object can be activated by the object as a cue to generate personal memories and evoke recollections of the past, as Proust's madeleine did for him. There is also an expressive, communicative element to the "object-toy", which is its capacity to relate to the world and tell what Polinoro calls "a story of relationships", "short fables... suggesting indirect links with play, and stimulating transposition into the fantastic."

This fantastic world suggested by Polinoro is inhabited by creatures of the imagination, all part of the crowd of characters gathering at the FFF party – some of the most recognisable products include a gas lighter called Firebird; a teapot called Penguin Tea; a coat peg named Antonio; Luca, the napkin holder in the form of a monster devouring the rolled fabric; Nutty the Cracker nutcracker and bowl with a polyamide squirrel; and a grinning devil of a bottle opener called the Diabolix. Possibly the most famous, Stefano Giovannoni's Merdolino is a toilet brush in thermoplastic resin. Alberto describes it best in *Art and Poetry*: "Toilet humour here takes the shape of a terracotta plant pot (in plastic of course) sprouting a curious green cactus." Such objects then became new channels for imaginative play, the instruments which we use for reaching out to others in newly creative ways.

At first glance, the alliterative, three-part name of the project does not seem to make much sense. Yet when we consider the importance of the role of imaginative play to the FFF, we begin to understand what the "Fiction" in the name means: "the construction of an imaginary world in which we can recognise ourselves, protects our innermost tenderness and creativity... objects are the new vehicles of imagination..." In other words, this metaproject tells stories and weaves narratives that have a validity of its own, which is tied indissolubly to a fragile, childlike part of us that must be safeguarded from harm. This innocent, familiar and familial dimension is what "Family" addresses: "[...] objects [...] create new 'families' [...] new places of recognisability and belonging; the capacity to build [...] the more intimate dimension of our identity as consumers." Put together, family does indeed follow fiction. The sense of kinship, of belonging to a larger network of relatives can only be felt when the imaginative capacity is enlarged to embrace the possibility that objects can touch people emotionally, just as kitchen devices can have personalities and sometimes, just sometimes, bathroom cleaning tools can become succulent shrubs.

Drawing by Stefano Giovannoni

1

2

3

1| *Ship Shape*, container
2| *Magic Bunny*, toothpick holder
3| *Nutty the Cracker*, nutcracker
4| *Mary Biscuit*, biscuit box
5| *Lilliput*, salt and pepper set
6| *Coccodandy*, basket for cooking eggs

113

1| *Alibaba*, jug with vacuum glass
2| *Happy Spices*, container/shaker
3| *Bunny & Carrot*, kitchen roll holder
4| *Mr Suicide*, bathtub plug with float
5| *Up-pill*, cotton pad dispenser
6| *Pino*, funnel
7| *Superpepper*, vegetable chopper
8| *Cico*, egg cup with salt castor
9| *Piripicchio*, clothes shaver

4

5

6

7

8

9

1| *Firebird*, electronic gas lighter
2| *Happy Spices*, container/shaker
3| *Pisellino*, cotton swabs holder
→ *Fruit Mama*, fruit holder with green polyamide tree

UNRELEASED PROTOTYPES

American sculptor, visual artist and body artist Vito Acconci's submission for the Tea & Coffee Towers project, which found residence in the Alessi hall of fame, remains one of the numerous prototypes that are unreleased. "True design," says Alberto, "isn't easy to handle." Although Alessi has successfully transformed countless abstract ideas and sketches into tangible objects, design and production do not always reach an agreement. For varied reasons and difficulties, these enigmatic prototypes that represent each designer's unique ideology never made it to the production stage. Nonetheless, these unrealised dreams create a growth for the company, as Alessi continues to seek possible solutions for the most impossible designs.

1| *Tea & Coffee Towers*, Vito Acconci, 2003
2| First prototypes of pieces made in stainless steel, Carlo Alessi, 1949
3| Folding chair, Aldo Rossi, 1987
→ Cheese grater, Luigi Fiorentino, 1996

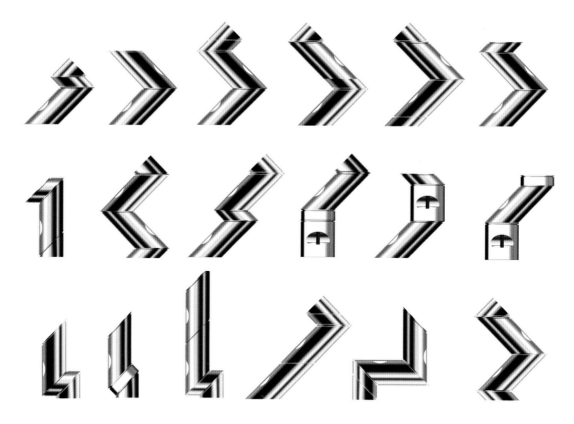

Tea & Coffee Towers, Shigeru Ban, 2003

Unreleased prototypes fall into the category of "neo-goods", a term coined by Denis Santachiara to describe design that straddles reality and utopia. His eccentric coffee maker, is a "neo-good" that is close enough to be manufactured, but too far off to be involved in inventive risks. Despite being perfectly functional, Santachiara's coffee maker is shaped horizontally and not vertically, hence upsetting the traditional logic of use. Its revolutionary design was shelved by Alessi because it supposedly belonged to a period where, as Patrizia Scarzella explains in *Steel and Style: The Story of Alessi Household Ware*, "the market is not ready to accept too innovatory items and is not yet sensible to the use or rediscovery of certain goods."

The designs of Vito Acconci and Shigeru Ban for the Tea & Coffee Towers fall into the same category of "neo-goods" as Santachiara's flat coffee maker. Entreating us to "start with a world [...] a self-enclosure [...] a world-in-itself", Acconci conjures up what Mendini has termed an "anthropological" contained sphere for his tea and coffee set, a literal sphere which is divided geometrically into four tetrahedrons, or pyramidal volumes, one each for coffee, tea, milk and sugar. Ban's tea and coffee set design evoked for Mendini an enigmatic "feeling of suspense created by a system of forms in a state of non-equilibrium". The two sets by Acconci and Ban were extremely complex and could compromise on

functionality if they were produced. To be precise, the Acconci set could have utilisation problems, whereas Ban's design suffered from problems to do with its stability. Similarly, Luigi Fiorentino's design of a cheese grater failed in the production process due to structural problems that could not be resolved by Alessi's technical department. In particular, the design of the cheese grater implied a fragile structure with its thin body. A stainless steel rod was then introduced to provide a stronger structure for Fiorentino's design, but the final result turned out to be a completely different object that did not respect the designer's intentions.

While these "neo-goods" were popularly acclaimed for their outstanding designs, some unreleased prototypes remained out of production because they emerged either too early or too late for their time. The first stainless steel prototypes, including the wire basket, were designed before Alessi started a major shift from using traditional metals of brass, nickel and silver to manufacturing in stainless steel. When the stainless steel production began in the 1950s, Alessi selected the brass products that could also be produced in stainless steel to be manufactured, and the first stainless steel prototypes, made in the late 1940s, remained unrealised. On the other hand, Aldo Rossi's design of the folding chair could have made it to production if it did not coincide with a similar project that another company was developing.

EXPERI-MENTAL PROJECTS

Bringing Alessi into uncharted territory is one tall order, but that was exactly where the Italian design factory intended to go when they initiated Treasure Box for Urban Nomads and the Tea & Coffee Towers. Risks and uncertainty are unavoidable, but in undertaking experimental projects, Alessi has given birth to groundbreaking ideas and bestsellers that reveal new perspectives on traditional household products. For Alberto Alessi, these avant-garde designs "represent desire, in other words, to pursue advanced research with a high degree of formal, constructive and functional innovation [...] free from the structures normally imposed by large-scale industrial production." Gary Chang's enthralling multi-functional receptacle and the 22 stunning micro-architectural services developed under the direction of Alessandro Mendini thus emerged.

The Tea & Coffee Towers project introduced a creative playground for 22 internationally acclaimed architects to explore design on a significantly smaller scale. It builds on the success and is a derivative of the 1983 Tea & Coffee Piazza project, for which architects designed silver services and exhibited them at an exhibition arranged by Hans Hollein. "Each of the designers found forms to express their styles and ideas, and in that period this operation revolutionised not only the general appearance of domestic objects but also some basic principles of design itself as a discipline", says Mendini, who spearheaded the enormous design effort. Made mainly from silver, 20 spectacular tea and coffee sets were produced in limited editions of 99 copies per design, with the prototypes of Vito Acconci and Shigeru Ban unrealised due to manufacturing complexities.

After Tea & Coffee Towers, Gary Chang went on to pursue another partnership with Alessi with an experimental project that moves "beyond the visual" of industrial design. Deceivingly simplistic, the design of Treasure Box for Urban Nomads deviates from the highly sophisticated household items exemplary of Alessi. Yet, the multi-functional storage item maintains the same "intellectual stimulation, surprise and aesthetic delight" that a praiseworthy design offers. What lit Chang's imagination for this project was a desire to create a Pandora's box for the modern, debonair globetrotter. On a practical level, Chang's masterpiece was cleverly designed to fit a home in a box, taking into account the spatial restriction that accompanies the avid traveller. A piece of luggage, a jewellery box, a coffee and tea set or a snack dish – Treasure Box for Urban Nomads is anything and everything you want it to be.

TREASURE BOX FOR URBAN NOMADS

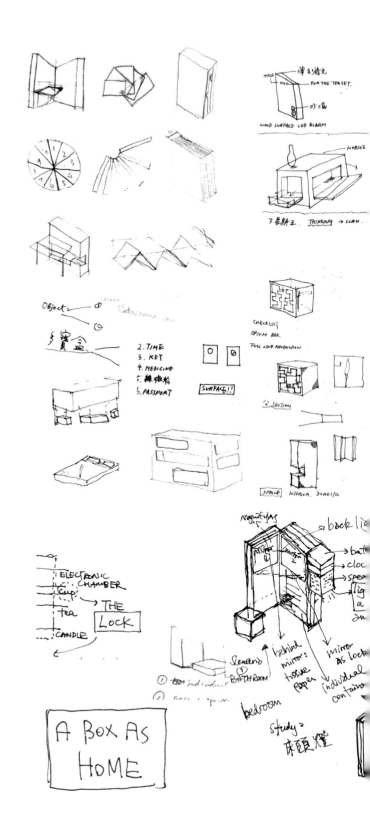

With a moniker as catchy and fantastical as this, the Treasure Box for Urban Nomads stirs up images of Bedouin nomadic wanderers and swashbuckling pirates. While the modern jet setting business traveller going from city to city may not lead lives of such dangerous glamour and epic proportion, the Treasure Box was designed to form an integral part of the 21st century globetrotter's lifestyle.

The limited edition item is several things at once; just some of its functions include luggage, jewellery box, furniture, tea set, stationery holder, game set and food dish. Made up of a series of compartments which can be folded into one compact box, it is fascinating for the myriad storage opportunities it offers as well as its ability to unfold in various ways and cater to specific needs.

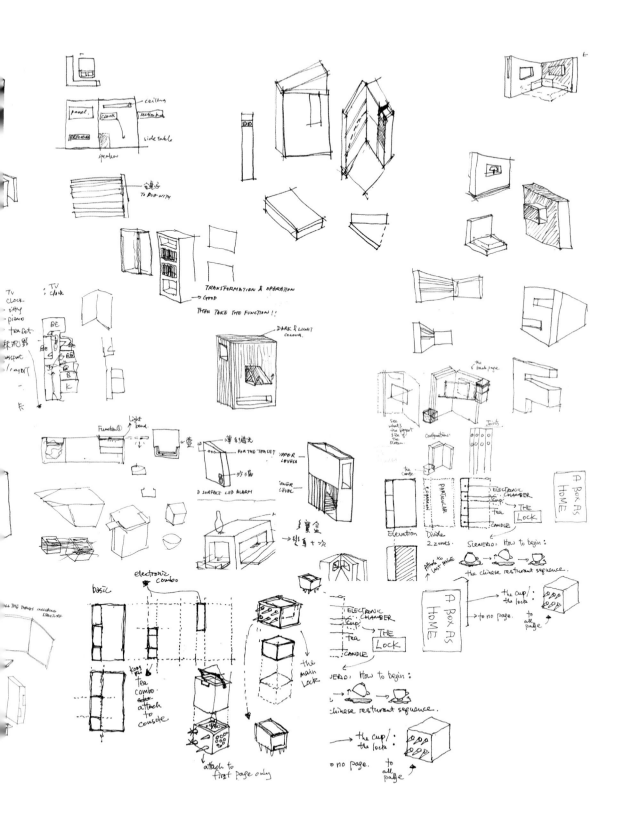

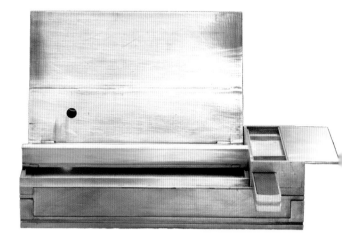

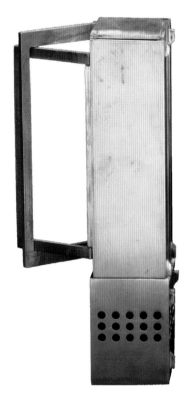

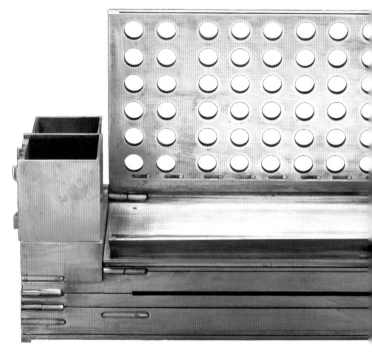

Can you tell us about the most fruitful dialogues between Alessi and yourself which gave birth to the final design?
One day Alberto said, "I know you are not into visual things!" It was a clear moment after we had collaborated for more than seven years that he firmly concurred with my key objective in whatever we are doing that we would really want to focus on things or considerations beyond the visual.

Alessandro Mendini's label for your Tea and Coffee Towers project is "a totem for the micro-domestic landscape". This can also be applied to the Treasure Box, which has in turn been described as "an interaction between your home and hotel". At the same time, it is an object that is highly architectural in its lines, design and execution. How does this one product negotiate the twin concern for on one hand, the hard structural lines of construction and on the other, its domestic and intimate function?
I am always provoking ideas to counter preconceptions of a very often over-simplified interpretation of things, such as wood equals warmth or metal means cold. We believe an object or an act could have various meanings depending on different circumstances and intentions.

In the case of The Treasure Box for Urban Nomads, I would not quarrel with the fact that precision in micro-environment can co-exist with intimacy. Take the example of a diamond ring. One cannot deny that it is both highly precise and intimate at the same time.

What was the inspiration for the Treasure Box? Why did you decide on copper as a material?
The idea of a Treasure Box for Urban Nomads was in my mind for a pretty long time ever since I became one of the "nomads", trying to squeeze everything into my hand-carry luggage irrespective of the durations of the trips. I even thought of designing my own luggage as I still could not find an ideal suitcase in the market. Very often, they are either too fancy or had too many gadgets which are far from practical.

Naturally, the inspirations of the Treasure Box are from the various similar objects found in many places, from China to France, and from Japan to Sri Lanka. I found that this is a universal interest, making a commodity possess both the characters of functionality and fun at the same time.

The choice of material of copper was actually more a suggestion from Alberto as we believe that would optimize the unique craftsmanship Alessi possess, and the fact that the box really demands ultra-high precision and minute details. Copper was the perfect candidate. The use of copper strangely enough imparts an air of antiquity to the final result even though it is pretty contemporary in intentions. This I found a happy accident!

The Treasure Box, much like your architectural works, manipulates space. Yet there is also an element of surprise, of pleasure, of an almost childish delight. From its name that brings to mind pirates and buried gold to its astonishing adaptability, it seems a very playful work.
To me, the most important task of design is to make every thing you need to do every day both perfect in execution and a game to play instead of doing trivial designs and products which are somehow "disposable". Sometimes I really have that feeling of objects being "over-designed" in the design profession as I have stated earlier.

Also, my inspiration for the Treasure Box came from a whole range of collectibles I have in my studio: the golden warrior Transformers from Japan, the ever-evolving multi-plug adaptors ... and of course the Lego which I have played with since childhood.

Yet despite this, it is also obviously extremely cerebral and its design is carefully thought out to maximise the functional possibilities. Would you say this was your philosophical approach for the Treasure Box? Playfulness balanced with controlled use of space?
I agree that this is the key intention of the project!

Gary Chang

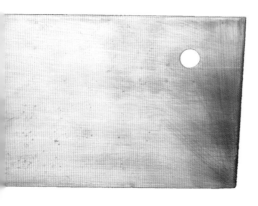

TEA & COFFEE TOWERS

The 1983 Tea & Coffee Piazza (TCP) project was born of a dream of the young Alessandro Mendini and Alberto Alessi. 11 architects were invited to design tea and coffee sets, in a revolutionary attempt to present a new alternative to Italian bel design, which was in decline by the late 1970s. At that time, Alberto felt that Alessi was "writing an important chapter in the history of contemporary design". The eventual birth of two of Alessi's all-time best-sellers, Aldo Rossi's La Conica coffee maker and Michael Graves' 9093 kettle proved that Alberto's intuition was spot-on.

Keen for a repeat of the phenomenal success of the TCP, Alessi launched the Tea and Coffee Towers (TCT) project in 1999, again under the stewardship of Mendini. The TCT's assembly of 22 illustrious international architects was given free rein to experiment and explore new ways to approach their domestic micro-architecture for the table. Their miniature towers of fancy in the form of the archetypal tea and coffee set crafted a different tabletop landscape. Merging breathtaking architectural elements with homely functionality, the TCT sought to bring Alessi's design factory to greater heights by tapping on the virtuosos of the 21st century architectural world.

The result was an exceptional collection of 22 sets that reflected the diverse and extraordinary imaginations of the designers. Wholly unpredictable and highly exclusive, the TCT was finalised in 2003 after three years in the making. Part of the Officina Alessi brand, prices were stratospheric to say the least, and were a reflection of what the sets represented apart from their intrinsic design merits. They were symbols of the collaboration between a firm highly-respected for their design sensibilities and architects who have designed some of the world's most remarkable buildings.

Yet not every single design went from sketchbook to production. Of the 22 designs, the production only consisted of the limited run of 20 tea and coffee sets, each of which 99 copies were released on the market. The final two projects from the TCT suffered a similar fate as some in the TCP – the difficulty of putting it into production. Some of the designs in 1983 were not fit for industrial production in a series. More than 20 years later,

Vito Acconci presented a design that was reminiscent of spacecrafts and science fiction settings. Deemed to have utilisation problems if made, the potential hitches were to do with its function; additionally, it was extremely complex to manufacture. The other prototype that was proposed but put on hold belonged to Japanese architect Shigeru Ban. According to Mendini, it was "a set of tubular objects cut at an angle and recomposed […] as if off balance on a plane surface." Experimenting with space and form, Ban's design was not functional for a different reason: it could not balance on its own.

The other 20 sets also were experimental, each in its own unique way. Some took a more cerebral approach in their interrogation of time and space, as with Tom Kovac, Greg Lynn, Thom Mayne, UN Studio and Zaha Hadid, amongst others. Some played with materials and forms, as Massimiliano Fuksas and Doriana O. Mandrelli did with their set that looked like a folded sheet; MVRDV's cylinder that looked pinched and squeezed; Jean Nouvel's gilded metal shell or Toyo Ito's pure white ceramic vessels with green frogs perched on the edges. Yet others wanted to impart feelings of beauty and surprise, as with Mendini's set made from carved wood that he calls the "joker in the pack"; SANAA's exquisite fruit basket and Gary Chang's "kung-fu teaset" that recalled the ancient Chinese ritual of the tea ceremony. Pleasure and desire were the motivations behind Will Alsop's and Dominique Perrault's sets, designed for the pleasure of savouring a cup of coffee or tea; while tradition and family were behind Dezsö Ekler's. Denton Corker Marshall's set, one of the most explicitly architectural, was inspired by skyscrapers. Juan Navarro Baldeweg's was colourful and played with height, as did Wiel Arets'. David Chipperfield's was simple, almost ascetic; while Future Systems' was simple and timeless in completely different ways.

The singularities are as many as the designers, and all the first prototypes were showcased to the public in the City of Towers exhibition, part of the Venice International Biennale of Architecture in 2002. Alberto was once again proven right, and the TCT was yet another important chapter in the book of design history that Alessi is continuing to write.

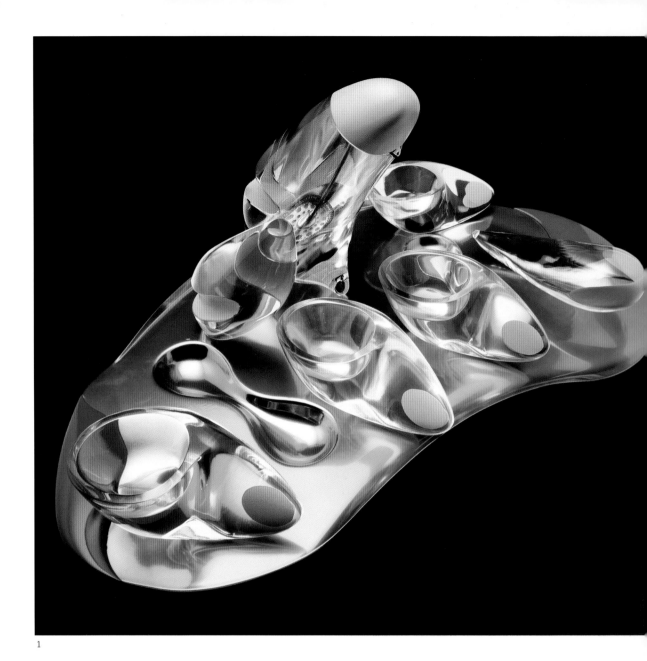

1

1| Future Systems
2| Denton Corker Marshall
3| Toyo Ito

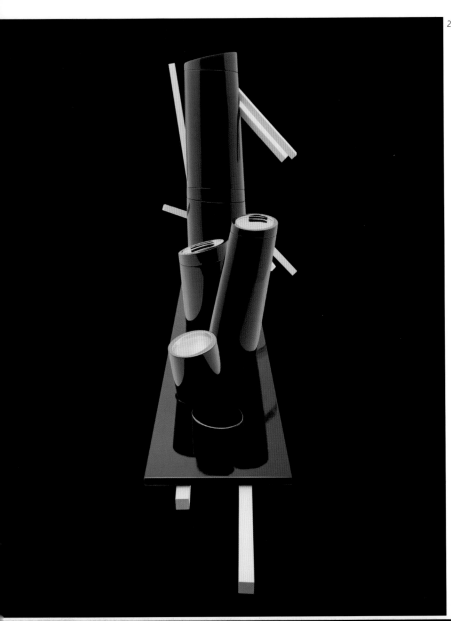

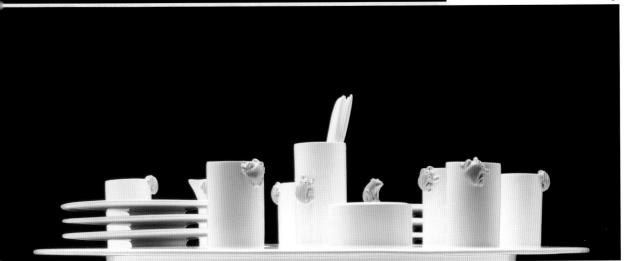

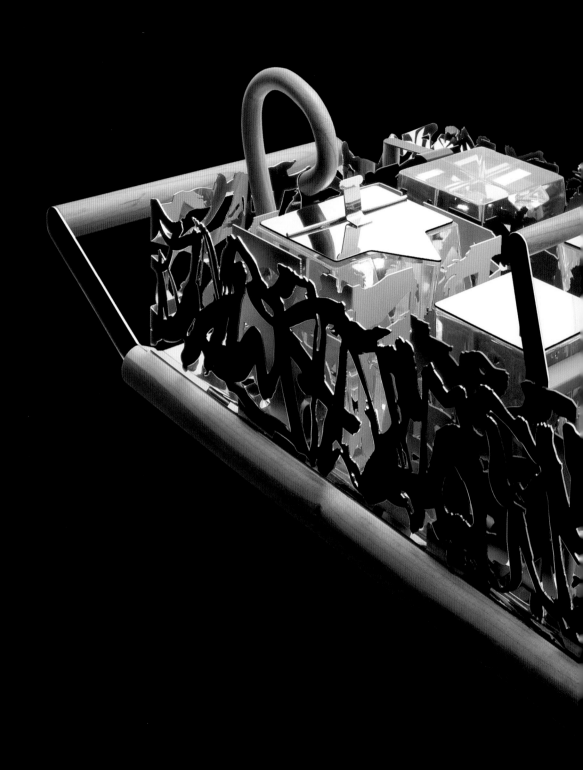

Juan Navarro Baldeweg

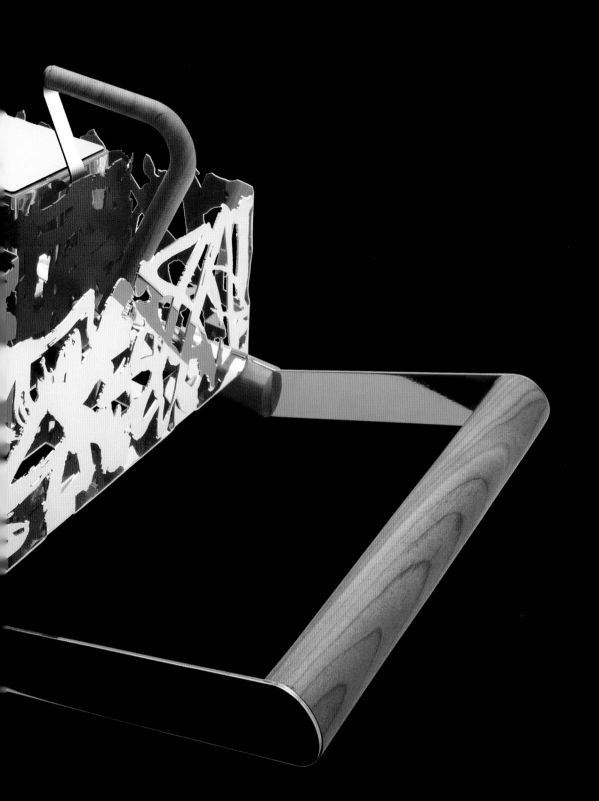

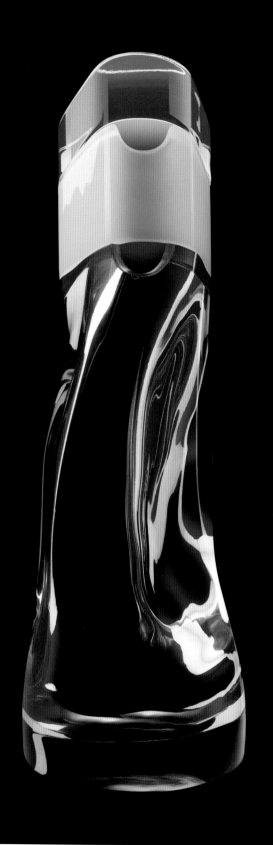

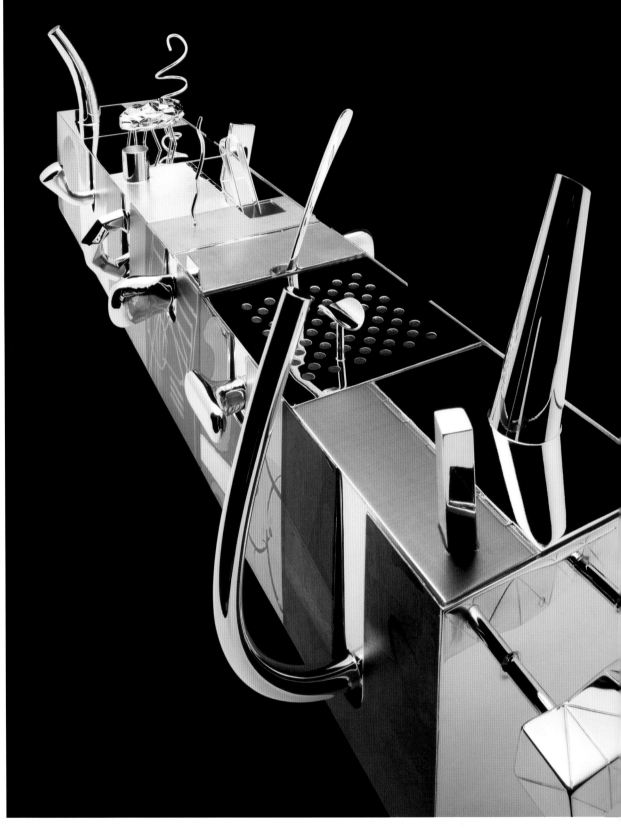

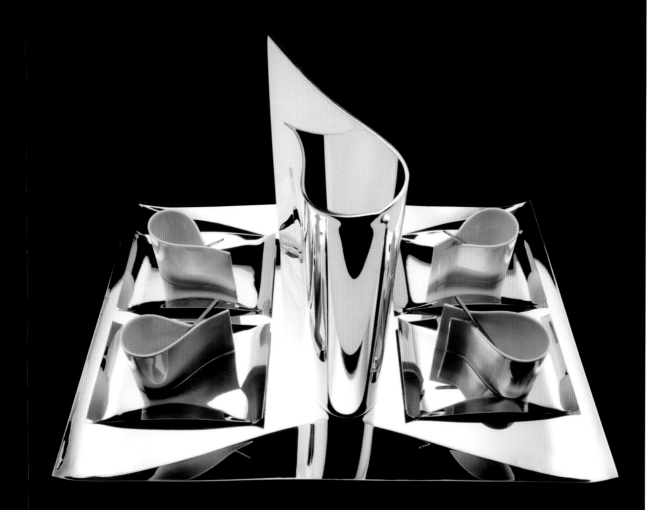

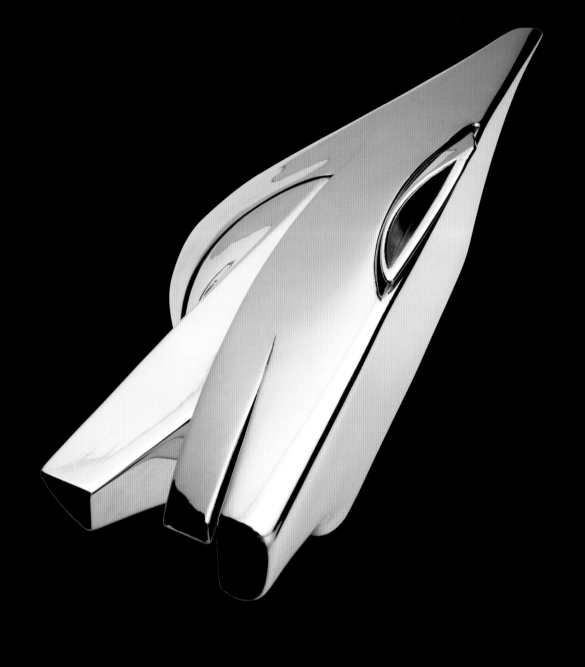

1| Gary Chang
2| Dominique Perrault
3| Dezsö Ekler
4| Zaha Hadid

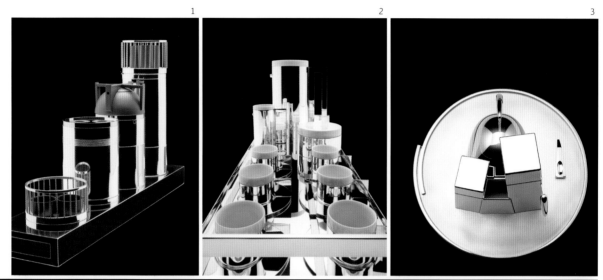

Tom Kovac

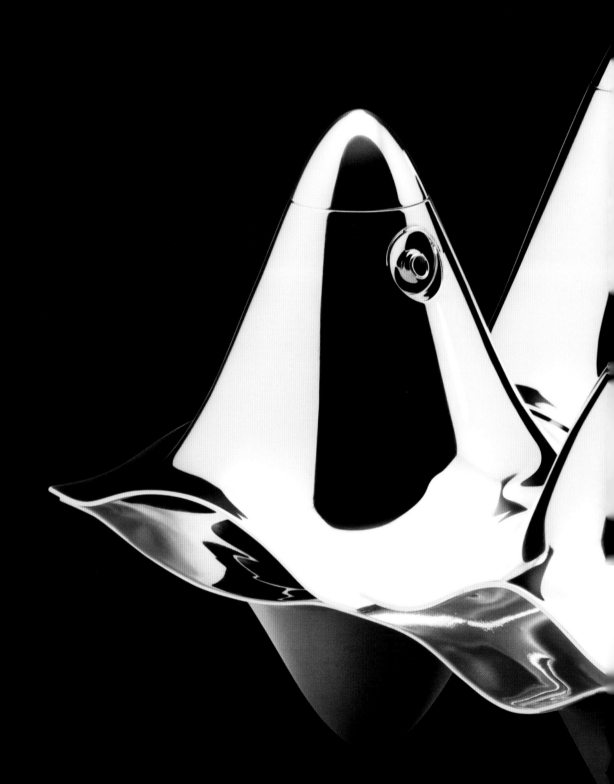

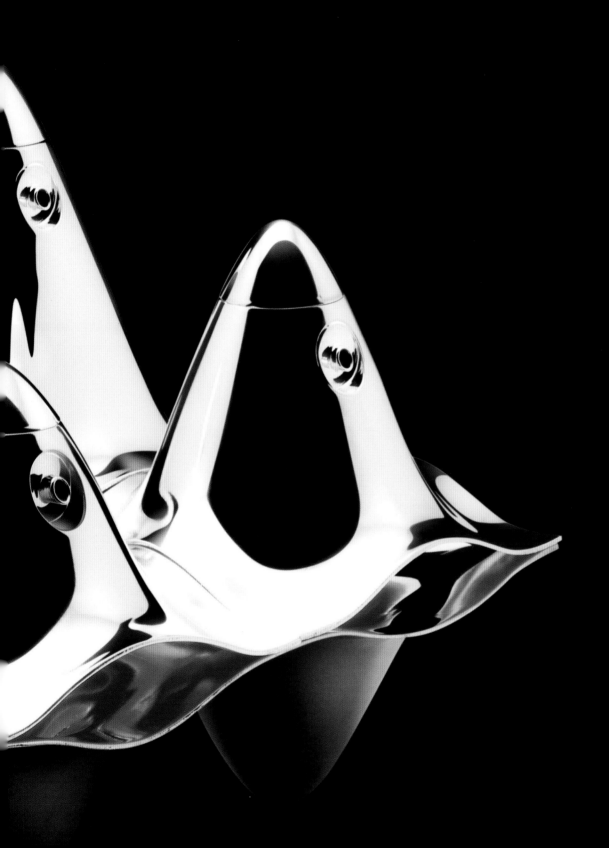

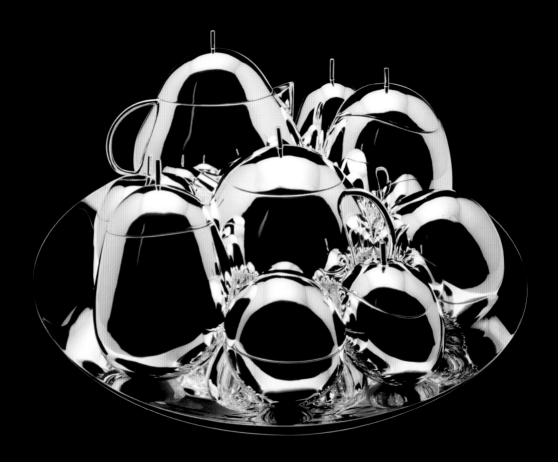

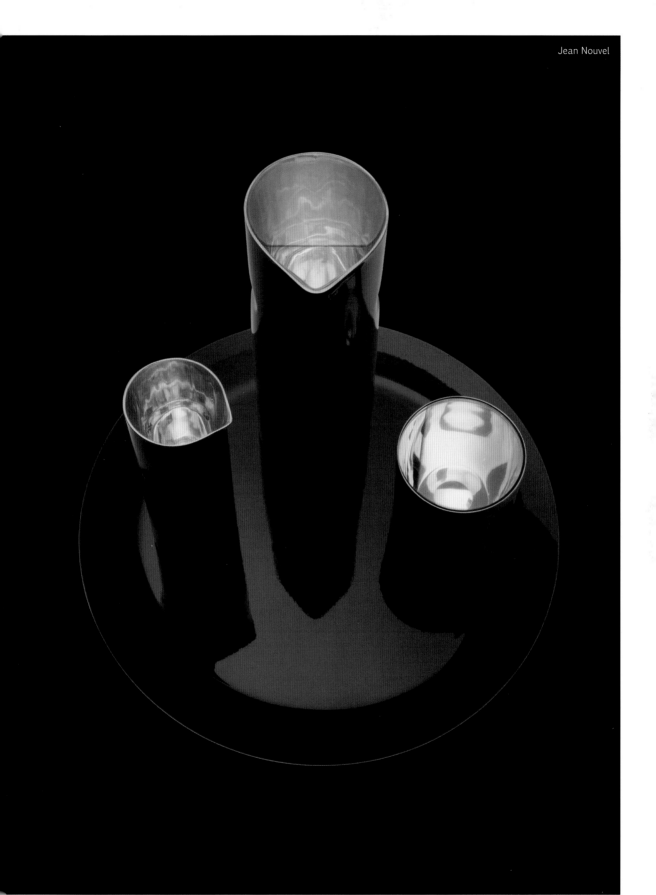

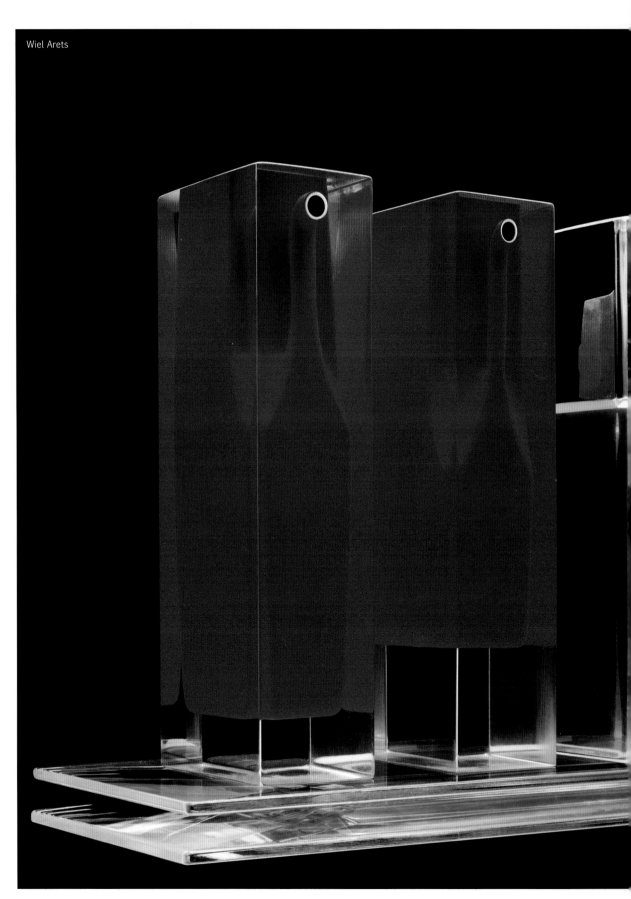

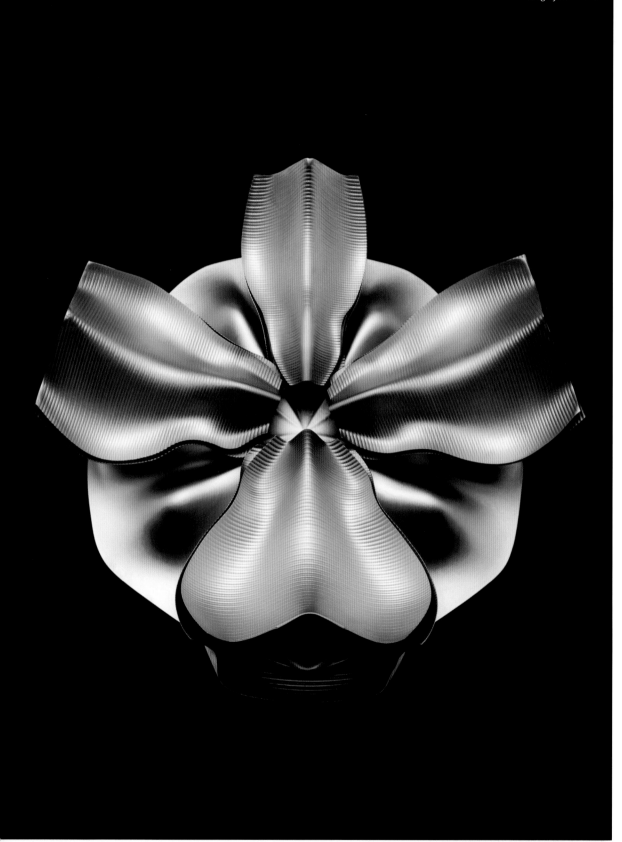

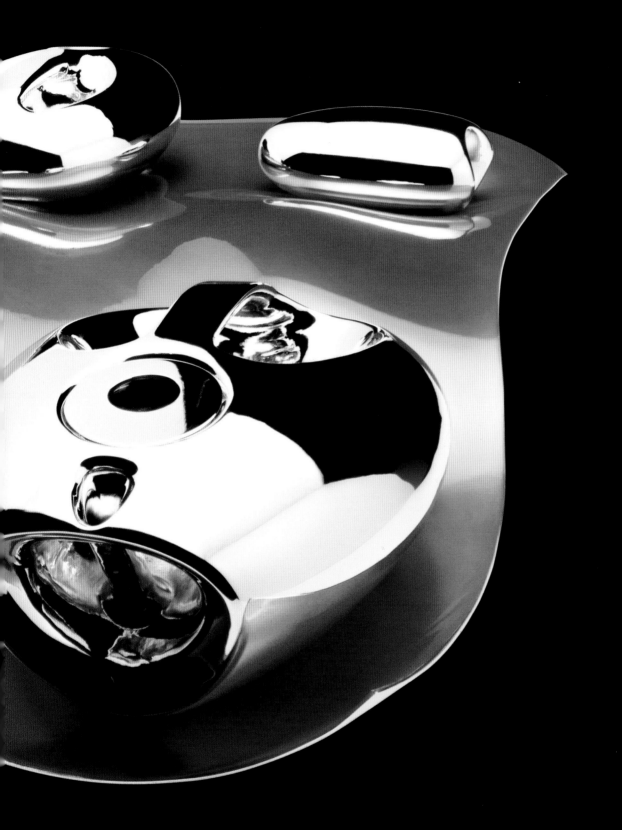

MUSEO ALESSI

"We call it a museum," says curator Francesca Appiani. "But it's not a museum, it's an archive." Certainly Museo Alessi is more than simply a faculty that showcases Alessi's design heritage since its beginnings in 1921. Possessing a vast body of 15,000 prototypes and 20,000 drawing sketches, the museum is, as Appiani further elaborates, "a three-dimensional encyclopaedia of kitchen and household typologies."

Being in a class of its own when it comes to Italian design and art, it is a well-known fact that Alessi's acclaimed masterpieces are housed in many museums' permanent collections, the likes of which include the MoMA, the Victoria and Albert Musuem and the Centre Pompidou. Yet, as Appiani mentioned, Museo Alessi is not your typical museum. Unusual as it seems, Museo Alessi's visitors are mainly Alberto and internal technical staff, and its compounds are open to visitors by reservation only. Located within the Alessi building in Crusinallo, this impressive library, chock-full of inspirations, memories, ideas and solutions of the Italian design factory, serves its quiet purpose as an all-in-one research centre for the entire Alessi team, including external designers. On a more basic level, the museum acts as a private workroom for Alberto and the staff to have easy access to all information regarding the history and development of each previous project released or unreleased.

Designed by Alessandro Mendini, the Alessi museum plays a crucial role in forming a valuable cross-section of the history, identity and dreams of the Italian design factory. "Alberto usually organises the first meeting with the designer at the Alessi Museum," shares Appiani. Walking through the seemingly endless shelves of fascinating works, one can get an immediate idea of the Alessi philosophy and its modus operandi. Deliberately estranged from mainstream museums, Alessi Museum presents the perfect stage for the legends of the past to work alongside today's design geniuses.

Such an enormous growing archive needs superior organisation. According to Appiani, the museum is specifically organised in order to "satisfy Alberto's requests and the needs of the technical department" when looking for materials, items and drawings. In every section, the pieces are arranged chronologically, and all unreleased projects from that particular category are placed at the end of every section. The museum constantly archives the history and development of every project past or present, including those that remain in suspension. Other than prototypes, design sketches, technical drawings and actual artefacts, Museo Alessi also files the creative dialogues between designers and Alessi, recording the stories, philosophy and approach behind each designer's work in the form of interviews.

But why call it a museum when it operates mainly as a tool for management and research? "We (do) run some museum activities and services," explains Appiani. Museo Alessi works closely with other traditional museums by providing loan and consultation services for private and public exhibitions. Each year, they receive about 30 loan requests for exclusive materials that can only be found in the Alessi archive. "Traditional design museums have the final products, while we have the work behind the final product," clarifies Appiani. With a plethora of materials, Museo Alessi can offer countless pieces of information from different points of views when they are approached with unique requests from researchers, journalists, museum curators or students. On certain occasions, Alessi also conducts temporary exhibitions and historical researches on their own collection.

For over ten years since its opening in 1998, this chamber of treasures containing Alessi's rich heritage has been a strong pillar of support for the company in its design endeavours. By progressively building upon the previous projects, Alessi believes that "this is the way to develop our ability to set trends, to promote our fame and to create a culture medium aimed at developing those projects we like to call super and popular," says Alberto. Without a doubt, this cabinet of curiosities, with the creative essences within its walls, will continue to grow in accordance with the company, inspiring greater innovation and experimentation of exemplary products so loved by people from all over the world.

THE DESIGNERS

The years under Carlo Alessi's management which spanned both wars saw the firm producing its very own designs of household items exclusively, with several pieces such as the Bombé set, the wire basket and the baroque tray, all achieving legendary commercial success. Ten years after the Bombé, Alessi's acquaintance with the young architects Luigi Massoni and Carlo Mazzeri resulted in the firm's venture outside of its own design field. Conceptualised by Massoni and Mazzeri, the shaker, the ice container and the drink cooler became the first products designed outside Alessi. The steel shaker, along with the set of bar accouterments, soon became a runaway hit, reaching manufacture figures of more than 500,000 units.

To this day, Alessi has collaborated with over 250 designers from all over the world, and their sympathy for designers is well-known. The designer of the bestselling Kalisto containers, Claire Brass, attests to this in an interview: "Designers are treated like gods when you are developing a project. They will do anything to get it right."

Since the first creative partnership in the 1950s, commissioned designers have stood on the cusp of the Italian design factory with their cutting edge contributions to Alessi. Like Jasper Morrison, one of Alessi's most important designers, the seven world-famous architects featured in this book represent one of the essential directions of Alessi's past and future. Among them, Wiel Arets, Toyo Ito, Sanana, Hani Rashid and Gary Chang are more recent partnerships, while Alessandro Mendini and Stefano Giovannoni are veteran collaborators and have been working with Alessi since the 1980s.

—WIEL ARETS

Laying eyes on Wiel Aret's earliest sketches for Alessi, Alberto Alessi believed he had found one of Alessi's design heroes for the new millennium. "Wiel Arets doesn't follow trends, nor can he be easily classified," writes Alberto, "His work tends towards a regularity of parts, without being minimalist in the reductive sense."

Unlike most of the architects who participated in Alessi's 2000 Tea and Coffee Towers project, the Dutch architect has extended his relationship with Alessi beyond designing kitchenware. His projects for Alessi include a watch, jewellery, a telephone and a bathroom range. For the Tea and Coffee set, Arets' distinctive design is in the form of solid blocks without spouts or handles, standardising the height for all vessels. Arets also designed the second bathroom range from Alessi. Focused on hygiene and relaxation, the timeless design of the Il Bagno Alessi dOt collection revolves around the shape of a circle and the purity of water as an element.

What was your response to Alessi's invitation to design for them?
Alberto called to ask if I would be interested in the Tea and Coffee project, as he saw that the project was a good collaboration with architects. I asked him why. He explained that he had seen my work and that I was an architect who has done industrial design. For Alessi, I had to think about people using a product and that challenged me a lot.

How would you describe Alessi as a client?
What I like about Alessi as a client was that they really talked to us and not simply asked questions. Alberto talked to me about the conceptual part of the project. He was a real client. Our collaboration was a cycle: first the idea, then the process and then the end product. I appreciate that about him. In the long run, the Alessi collection has a consistency in terms of conceptual strength. Everyone is producing their own thing, but Alberto is the constant factor in all of Alessi's work. That is very rare and different from other firms. For all the projects I have done with Alessi, the process is the same. We always talked about it from beginning to end.

To you, what is the essence of Alessi's design philosophy?
Their choice of architects demonstrates their philosophy. They select their architects very carefully, since the architect will not change his philosophy, and then give them a lot of freedom. They stimulate the architects to produce and design with total freedom. They have never said, you cannot do this or you cannot do that.

Alessandro Mendini describes your work on the Tea and Coffee Towers as having "a flavour of primordial technicism". What were some of the most fruitful dialogues with Alessi which gave birth to the final designs?
Mendini is someone who has worked with Alessi for a long time and who has brought the company a lot of recognition. He was interested in my work and wanted to know more about my ideas. The debate I had with him started when I made a sketch of my ideas for the Tea and Coffee Towers with the glass container. The tower as an architectural structure is very big, compared to the scale of the Tea and Coffee Towers, but he immediately saw the similarities despite the difference in scale.

How did you translate your design philosophy and expertise as an architect to the specific requirements of designing a product on a small scale for Alessi?
I see many similarities. Both have a programme, users, scale, and most importantly, both start out of a concept, be it designing for a room, or a building, or an industrial product. It's about the concept. This applies to both the design as architecture and the design as a product.

What were your considerations in designing the way your Tea and Coffee set would interact with the user?
I wanted to produce something contemporary and also infused with symbolism and functionalism. The container contained the fluid with the handle much like the way a milk carton is held. I came up with a simple solution of the artificial glass as a handle. The spout is symbolic because the spout is something that is universally understood, something that people have an impression of what it is. The spout has been used in Egypt for 4,000 years and it is essential because the problem is how to get the hot fluid into a cup. We needed a spout.

What opportunities did working with different media in industrial design present, especially in terms of expressing your attentiveness to texture?
The difference between an industrial product and an architectural product (which is exposed to rain and weather elements) is something that's interesting to me. I think about design in a different way from how I think about an architectural project. The idea of hygiene struck me deeply. Because you have to clean these products, the idea changes. The surface of industrial projects becomes interesting. The artificial glass is a medium to contain the liquid inside. I used silver and Japanese lacquer inside the glass, which on the outside is both smooth and hygienic. My attention is on how people will clean a bathroom. It's a terrible thing when the bathroom is not clean. The bathroom is about the cleanliness of the body; a physical and psychological cleanliness. It also has to do with meditation – the relationship between the user and product. I would describe it as hygiene.

What do you think of Alessi moving beyond the kitchen and into the realm of the bathroom with the Il Bagno Alessi projects?
Alessi has everything to do with the house. The kitchen has changed dramatically from what it was 50 years ago. The bathroom has changed even more. Hence, everything has to be designed, not just the basin, shower, but the entire range. The bathroom today is different. The project with Alessi made me re-think the short history of the bathroom – how it is now part of the house and how to deal with that. The bathroom is now a total concept. The borders now are blurred between different parts of the house.

The standardising of sizes within the Tea and Coffee Towers set and Il Bagno Alessi are part of your efforts to remove "a sense of hierarchy". What lies behind your interest in standardisation and uniformity in your design?
The four pieces in my Tea and Coffee Towers set are of the same height and size. I believe strongly in differences and I believe in rules. The moment I design the bathroom, all surfaces are flat with the idea of making everything as flat as possible. The element of the circle was something I tried to give all the products; I tried to treat them as the same thing. You can call it democracy or a lack of sense of hierarchy. The same rules apply when I design a series of 72 pieces. When I design the first five or nine pieces, every time I reach the ninth, tenth or 11th piece, or even the 50th piece, I have to go back to the first piece. I understand that for all 72, the rules are the same. The functions are different, but the design rules have made them into one family. It's a complicated thing, very complicated, but also a lot of fun.

1| left ▶ right: *screw.it*, corkscrew | *salt.it*, salt grinder |
pepper.it, pepper mill, 2008

2| *Il Bagno Alessi dOt*, 2007

→ *coffee.it*, electric espresso coffee maker, 2008

1

—*TOYO ITO*

A leader in postmodern Japanese architecture, Toyo Ito has designed two ranges of products for Alessi. The first is the celebrated Tea and Coffee Towers in 2003, a clean, simple set of white ceramic cups, saucers and holders embellished with green ceramic frogs perched delicately at the rims. The Tea and Coffee Towers project is inspired by ripples in water pools, and embodies uncomplicated ceremonial beauty and purity. Ito has also designed Ku, his maiden attempt at designing a mass-produced product. A porcelain table set complete with plates, salad bowls, mugs, cups and saucers, the delightful twist in the Ku collection arrives in the special version of the coffee cup and mug, where a ear-shaped handle replaces the more conventional handle.

Ku collection, mug, 2006

What was your response to Alessi's invitation to design for them?
I felt that we shared a common design philosophy. This is not only limited to their sophisticated design, but also their wit and concern for pricing within the reach of the general public.

How would you describe Alessi as a client and the way they work with designers?
Alessi is wonderful; they are full of wit and have excellent taste. I feel a great sympathy with them because Mr. Alberto Alessi's personal taste pervades every aspect of the work. They listen to our ideas and requests until the end, and they show strong understanding from the standpoint of designers.

How would you describe the Alessi brand?
The Alessi brand has vividness just like how true Italians enjoy life. I believe that architecture and design must brighten and please people. Italians, who enjoy drinking good wine, eating delicious food and dressing up, make the most of their lives, overflowing with good spirit. Alessi symbolises this spirit.

Where do your thought processes begin when designing for Alessi?
My thought process begins by using other designers' products for Alessi. The designs of Hoffmann, Castiglioni and Sottsass are particularly impressive, and I can learn a lot about the meaning of design. In the 20th century, under the influence of the Modernist era, design flourished greatly. I can feel such a blossoming of exciting energy and spirit in design from Alessi's products, and it gives me great courage and vitality.

Alessi sees itself as "mediators between the expression of creativity and the real things that touch people's hearts". How have Alessi's products influenced their customers' lives?
I find Alessi's tableware and other products to be wonderful and classic design that can be used daily.

To you, what is the essence of Alessi's design philosophy?
To design the joy of daily life. As I mentioned before, to eat, dress and live are fundamental activities of human life. To design objects related to our living is nothing less than to express the joy of life.

Water is the theme of your architecture and you have translated the water element in your design for the Tea and Coffee Towers. Frogs also, you write, allude to water. Why has this element inspired you?
From ancient times, humans have lived on the banks of good water. We take in water and release it, and our bodies are like the branches of a river. The people of the world are bound together by water.

You used white ceramics for the design of Tea and Coffee Towers to represent blank spaces that spread infinitely. In contrast, the images of the frogs on the cups are playful and embodied. How do the two materials and images work together?
By abstracting the cups and saucers to be as simple as possible, the cuteness and liveliness of the frog are emphasised.

You also designed a porcelain table set for Alessi, one of your first mass-produced projects. What considerations did you factor in when designing this set?
I intended to express the traditional softness of Japanese tableware and the space which spreads infinitely.

Which of the two cup versions for the set do you prefer – the more classical one or the one with an ear-shaped handle?
I prefer the ear-shaped handle because I find it humorous and delightful.

What is your opinion of the products you designed for Alessi and how they will stand the test of time?
I myself cannot know, but I hope that they will stand the test of time. I always wish the same for my architecture too.

↑ *Ku* collection, 2006
→ *Tea & Coffee Towers*, 2003

Ku collection, 2006

—*KAZUYO SEJIMA & RYUE NISHIZAWA (SANAA)*

Amongst the most exciting architecture firms known internationally, SANAA's work is recognised for its luminosity and Modernist simplicity. Their 2003 Tea and Coffee Towers set for Alessi was hailed by Alessandro Mendini as "an unlikely basket of high and subtle poetry, at the same time intellectual, feminine and fabulous". A tray of globular fruit forms made of silver resting on a stainless steel tray, the set employs SANAA's distinct style of understated sophistication in a non-hierarchical space. The duo has ensured each item in the set – a teapot, coffee pot, sugar bowl, milk jug sweet box and tray – rest comfortably side by side in a quirky but unexpectedly beautiful arrangement.

What were your responses to Alessi's invitation to design for them?
We felt very honoured. We remember how fun it was to go see Alessi's factory for the first time.

How would you describe Alessi as a client and the way they work with designers?
The design team we worked with had a deep understanding of design. They were very generous and we felt they must be one of the best partners to collaborate on design work. Reactions and responses were fast and accurate, and when we requested some things, they came back to meet with us with very accurate full-scale mock-ups. We were amazed at the speed and accuracy of these mock-ups. Also, they were very positive and objective about changes in designs. We appreciate their attitude and we feel we learned a lot working with them. We think that it has been a great collaboration.

Alberto Alessi has described SANAA's work on the Tea and Coffee Towers as "a new approach to design for the Alessi of the 20th century", quoting Toyo Ito's comments that your work "depends in the purest and simplest way on abstract spatial forms". What were some of the most fruitful dialogues between SANAA and Alessi which gave birth to the final designs?
It is difficult to say … but we appreciated how Alessi was generous and open to listen to our design ideas without being biased by their own knowledge in product design. It was inspiring for us to receive such positive responses.

How would you describe the Alessi brand?
It is a brand with a long history and is also modern at the same time. There have been many big hits among their products and we can relate to the various famous products. Alessi is one of the Italian makers well known not only among architects, but also by the general public.

Alessi sees itself as a "mediators between the expression of creativity and the real things that touch people's hearts". How, in both your opinions, have Alessi and its products influenced their customers' lives?
We totally agree with the quote. We have owned several Alessi products before we started to work together with Alessi and we enjoyed using them.

To you, what is the essence of Alessi's design philosophy?
Alessi products are produced for the table, kitchen or living room, and they give people hints to enjoy everyday life.

As architects, how did the both of you translate your design philosophy and expertise to the specific requirements of designing a product on a small scale for Alessi?
We tried to realise products with qualities that were small, light and cute and inspire people to see the future in industrial design.

What inspired the rounded globular fruit forms of the Tea and Coffee Towers?
The biggest influence is from shapes of real fruit pieces which are very cute and unique. Each piece is of a different shape, each has its own character and form. However, when they are gathered, some kind of harmony is born and they become a unique unit as a whole. The reflective qualities and sensitivity of stainless steel and silver also influenced the final design that we ended up with.

What were SANAA's considerations of how the Tea and Coffee set would interact with the user?
We hoped the products that appeared on the breakfast table could be used not just functionally but also be attractive objects on the table.

What is your opinion of the set you designed for Alessi and how it will stand the test of time?
Since they are made with stainless steel, they would not be damaged badly as other products. But as people use them, we hope they form a harmonious relationship with other kitchen goods.

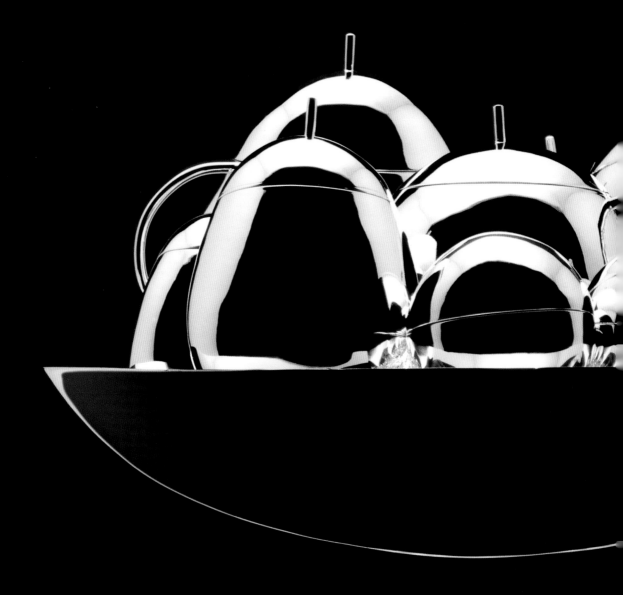

Tea & Coffee Towers, 2003

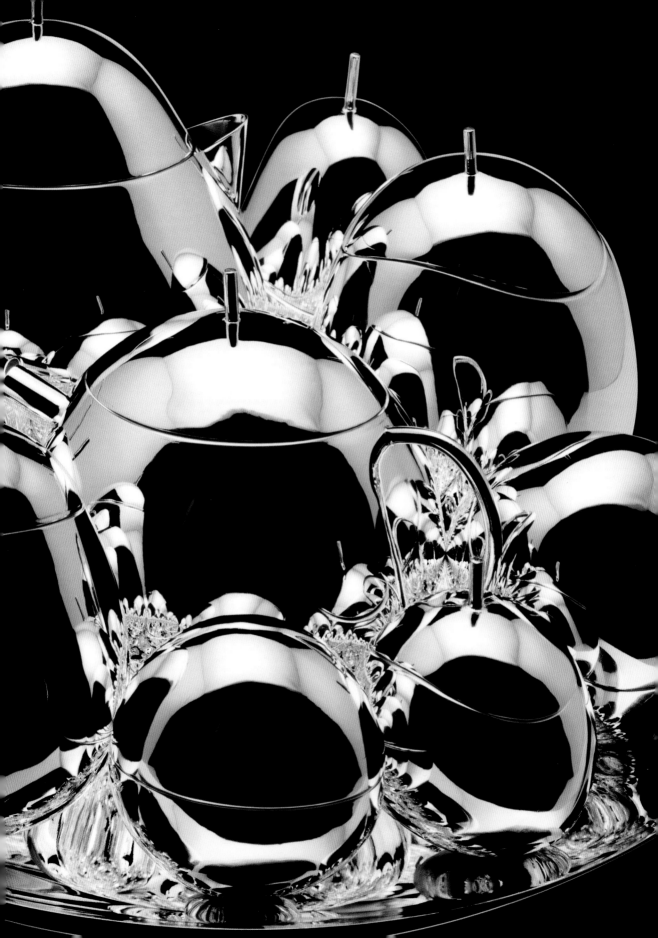

—HANI RASHID

Hani Rashid's collaboration with Alessi began in 2006 with the set of office stationery he calls Desktop Architecture, reflecting his academic background and part of Alessi's move to broaden their range beyond the kitchen. That same year, he introduced the Express Mocha collection made of bone china. He is also the designer of the much-acclaimed and high-profile Alessi flagship store in New York's SoHo district. The store houses a mirrored wall, experimental lighting installations that manipulate the spatial dimensions of the store, and a display concept which opens up new possibilities of displaying Alessi's products. Coupled with the first coffee bar in an Alessi store, the project has won several awards including the Lumens Award of Merit.

*Your relationship with Alessi began
with the Desktop Architecture range in
2006. What was your response to Alessi's
invitation to design for them?*

I was extremely pleased that Alberto
invited me to work with Alessi in 2006.
I had long admired the company and, in
effect, grew up on Alessi products and was
always impressed and intrigued by the art
historical trajectory of the Alessi brand
in the late 20th century under Alberto's
impetus and auspices, especially as the
brand related to architects and architecture.
I developed the idea for Desktop
Architecture as an acknowledgment to the
important works of Aldo Rossi for Alessi.
Rossi had transferred his profound ideas
from his famous 1966 book *L'architettura
della città* into objects for Alessi. I thought
it appropriate to revisit this idea and
thereby transferred my own concepts and
ideas for new forms of urban architecture
to the scale and utility of objects. My
focus from the onset with Alessi was to
revive the cultural pedigree of the brand
towards architecture. The power of the
Alessi brand, to my mind, is in its ties to
architecture and not necessarily design.
The iconic objects that stemmed from
profound collaborations between Alessi
and the iconoclasts of 20th century design
and architecture all centered around a
curious intersection of design, architecture
and art, and it was this aspect that I took to
when designing the products and stores for
Alessi as a part of its 21st century trajectory.

*How would you describe Alessi as a client
and the way they work with designers?*

They are a well-seasoned company with
regard to working with architects and
designers, that is certain. What struck me
at first as painfully "slow" procedures and
feedback became a luxury of sorts for me,
and through the process of working with
Alberto, Danilo and others, I began to
understand that the slowness was integral
to the creation of true quality in every
respect, from thinking to manufacturing.
In a nutshell, I would describe working
with Alessi as somewhere between needing
the patience of a medieval monk coupled
with a being a driver on a Formula One
circuit. In other words, my desire to turn
corners with even greater agility and speed
is well tempered by their desire to have an
espresso and talk about the curve ahead.

*What were some of the most fruitful
dialogues between Alessi and yourself
which gave birth to the final designs?*

We had many, many meetings which,
as I said, were enlightening and eye-
opening. The discussions that were the
most interesting to me in the process were
the simple ones, the ones where Alberto
himself would light a cigarette and ponder
an object for its beauty, utility and novelty,
then see either its essence and purpose, or
discard it without too much deliberation.
These moments fascinated me because they
occurred in between discussions on the
advent of computer-aided manufacturing,
steering clear of fashion and fads, new
materials and their properties and mass
production versus craft.

How would you describe the Alessi brand?

The Alessi brand is one that carries the
pedigree and DNA of architectural history.
The brand stands for sophisticated "out
of the box" utility and design that, more
often than not, is curious, beautiful and,
at times, strange and surreal. All told, this
makes for a brand that stands far above
competitors that only privilege some aspect
of design, be that utility, use of colour, or
symbolic forms and anecdotal design.

*Alessi sees itself as a "mediators between
the expression of creativity and the real
things that touch people's hearts". How
have Alessi and its products influenced
their customers' lives?*

The notion of designing artefacts for
people's homes and lives has to go beyond
mere utility and function. People need to
feel an affection for their objects and places
and that is where architecture and design
come in, providing a "metaphysical" and
poetic set of readings, associations and
beauty to enhance one's life. Alessi does
that in all of its output and their designers,
I believe, work from this foundation.

*To you, what is the essence of Alessi's
design philosophy?*

Beauty, function and enigma produce
objects of desire and affection.

*How did you translate your design
philosophy and expertise as an architect
to the specific requirements of designing a
product on a small scale for Alessi?*

Industrial design, one must remember,
was born from architecture: bending
tubular furniture, using new materials,
and so on, are all staples of early modern
design stemming from architects working
in various realms and using "design" of
products and furnishing to "test" materials
and methods. Today, with computing
and new manufacturing techniques and
materials, the story continues and, for me
personally, entering that story was the
means by which to navigate that world.

*What inspired the unusual forms of
the Desktop Architecture and the wavy
lines and almost awkward handle of the
Express Mocha Collection?*

I am not an industrial designer nor do I
have ambitions to be one. As an architect,
I saw and performed all of my design work
for Alessi as architectural experiments,
that is to say, as small spatial and material
ideas tested at a scale of domestic utility.
The Paper Trays, for example, are a model
for a building that we are designing in
the Emirates and the wavy lines were
called up from dealing with the poetics
and architecture of dunes and seascapes.
The handles of the espresso cups are
more walls and fins of a circular envelope
than functional handles for an espresso
cup. It so happens (and this comes from
the Surrealist tendencies I tend to work
from) that a small fin wall could be held
delicately in one's hand and assist in the
sipping of espresso.

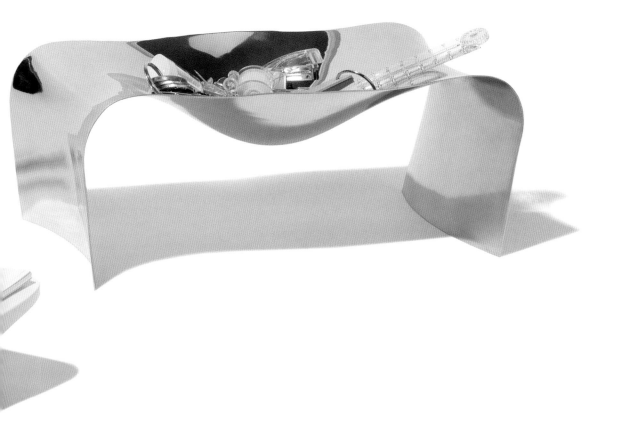

Desktop Architecture, 2006

—GARY CHANG

Gary Chang's collaboration with Alessi began in 2000 with the Tea and Coffee Towers project. Inspired by his grandfather who used to perform the ritual of preparing Chinese tea, the Hong Kong-based architect designed his own Kung-Fu Tea Set. The parallels of the project with Chang's architectural practice are apparent in his exploration of "hyper-density and intensity". Employing the system of organisation in Chinese dim sum, tiny morsels of food placed in bamboo baskets piled up high, the design of the tea set comes in stackable containers executed in sterling silver and Yixing red clay, the unglazed material used in traditional Chinese tea ware. In 2008, Chang unveiled his latest design for Alessi, Treasure Box for Urban Nomads. A travelling case no bigger than an A5 sheet of paper, it multitasks as a case for travel essentials as well as a snack dish.

You began working on the Tea and Coffee Towers for Alessi in 2000. What was your response to Alessi's invitation to design for them?

When I received the invitation from Alberto with a project brief from Alessandro Mendini, I wondered why they chose someone from Hong Kong. Was it because of the year 1997, which put Hong Kong onto the world's centre stage? Was it because of our installation at the 7th Venice Biennale in June that same year? We had created a structure inspired by two special phenomena in Hong Kong – Cageman, depicting the cramped living conditions in the city, and Portland Street Brothels Lightscape, a notorious red-light district. Our local tourism board does not dare to mention these as they are appraisals of the cultural scene in Hong Kong. A quick analysis of the list of invited architects on the same letter revealed the fact that out of the 20 or more architects, only four were Asian and three out of four from Japan. I have not asked Alberto or Mendini about that. Somehow I would love to keep it as a mystery!

How would you describe Alessi as a client and the way they work with designers?

Through my eight years of collaboration with Alessi, it was more like meeting with friends than a client. Every time I met with Alberto at the Alessi headquarters, I had the luxury of a long chat with him and his colleagues, often with an overall review of the project in the morning, followed by lunch, feedback and more brainstorming in the afternoon. These sessions progressed from the office to the canteen, very often ending the discussion in Alberto's room. Sometimes, we discussed possibilities in the morning and I was totally astonished that after lunch, some brief prototypes in the form of simple metal structures were already made for discussion! I am not sure whether I am the exception. I have to admit the only time that I was asked to modify our design was to reduce the number of parts in the Kung-Fu Tea Set. In the end I did it (symbolically) – I took out the bowl for gelatos (I always enjoy having gelatos with tea!). They were mostly very patient in listening to my stories and I deeply felt a strong sense of mutual respect that I found really rare! We were seldom hurried to meet deadlines. Perhaps Hong Kong designers are too used to fast-track projects. Collaborating with Alessi was like

"slow design" in the positive sense. It is a bit of a happy joke that it took us three years to develop the Kung-Fu Tea Set from inception to production, while it took us a mere 16 months to complete a 140-metre high-rise project in Hong Kong.

What were some of the most fruitful dialogues between Alessi and yourself which gave birth to the final designs for the Tea and Coffee Towers?

We discussed the central theme of my Tea and Coffee Towers contribution, which was the subject of "hyper-density and intensity", not in a city, but on a table. Many people have a misconception that high density is an Asian phenomenon, but I argue that this is a global one. For example, I was having a dinner with a Greek professor one evening in Paris. He recommended a tiny restaurant, one of the oldest in Paris and very popular. I remembered having dinner rubbing shoulders with our fellow diners! The table was so tiny that it barely accommodated the Western rituals of forks and knives on the table, not to mention the other elements. So I proposed that my set to be a kind of a hyper-dense domestic landscape. I believe this is the main reason for the design being approved unanimously. There was another evening when Alberto invited me to dinner at his house. He asked if I was interested to design a cutlery set. I surprised him by saying that I sometimes thought the most useful cutlery sets were the ones you could get for less than one euro at the supermarket! I expressed to Alberto that we might be over-designing things. Instead, I proposed to design a table container for cutlery sets, something like the ones we see in food stalls or wonton noodle shops. Alberto expressed that he understood what I meant and he would think seriously about this.

What about the project Treasure Box for Urban Nomads?

One day Alberto said, "I know you are not into visual things!" It was a clear moment in our collaboration after more than seven years that he firmly concurred with my key objective: in whatever we are doing, we would really want to focus on considerations beyond the visual.

How would you describe the Alessi brand?

It is like a family of multiple characters – seniors in the family who ensure continuity in traditional craftsmanship as well as important designs and innovations, and juniors who keep on exploring new frontiers of design, eager to meet and work with new "friends". This family is expanding all the time. Though this family is Italian in origin, it grows to include places and identities beyond physical boundaries.

Alessi sees itself as a "mediators between the expression of creativity and the real things that touch people's hearts". How has Alessi and its products influenced its customers' lives?

Alessi products have the charm of adding value to daily essentials, which are by and large rare in domestic products, or are pioneers that influence the market. These values are multiple, be they emotional, sophisticated, or humorous.

To you, what is the essence of Alessi's design philosophy?

An open-minded approach in exploring new ways to enrich mundane elements and commodities of our ordinary daily lives.

Alessandro Mendini has described your work on the Tea and Coffee Towers as a "skyscraper tea set". How did you translate your design philosophy and expertise as an architect to the specific requirements of designing a product on a small scale for Alessi?

I would define architecture as training on the awareness of the environment, be it on the macro scale of urban planning or on a micro scale of small objects. Deep down, they are not that different; we have historically been too obsessed with categorisation. I always believe it is more useful to spend more time exploring how things are similar instead of how things are different. So, it would be fascinating to explore our ideas in architecture and apply it to the tea set. The theme of Tea and Coffee Towers taps into the implications of current urban issues and on the notions of density of urban space and intensity of activities. We try to employ our ideas that deal with architectural projects – the emphasis on change, choice, co-existence and connectivity.

What inspired you to combine the Chinese elements of dim sum and yum cha on the Tea and Coffee Towers, a project which has its roots in Western or specifically Italian design culture?

I have to admit I do deliberately try to make use of this rare opportunity to bring in Chinese culture into the project, that of dim sum and yum cha. At the same time, we try to avoid drawing reference only to the visual parallels. We are focusing, in the case of dim sum baskets, on the system of flexibility and of storage on a high-density "tablescape". Whereas for yum cha, my family is from Chiu Chau, and it seems not too many people, especially in the Western world, are familiar to the art of Kung-Fu tea, so this project has a hidden agenda to introduce this classical Chinese tradition.

"Ritual", "ceremony" and "icon" are words frequently used to describe your contribution to the Tea and Coffee Towers. You have said that it is "a totem for the micro-domestic landscape". What lies behind your interest in rituals and phenomena?

I believe that in the complex modern world, people are bombarded with too many things to do and too many distractions to deal with. In the end, one will discover that one simply cannot do too many things. As a result, most of the time, the genuine quality of things are gradually very much compromised. That's why we would like to re-introduce the notions of daily rituals and phenomena.

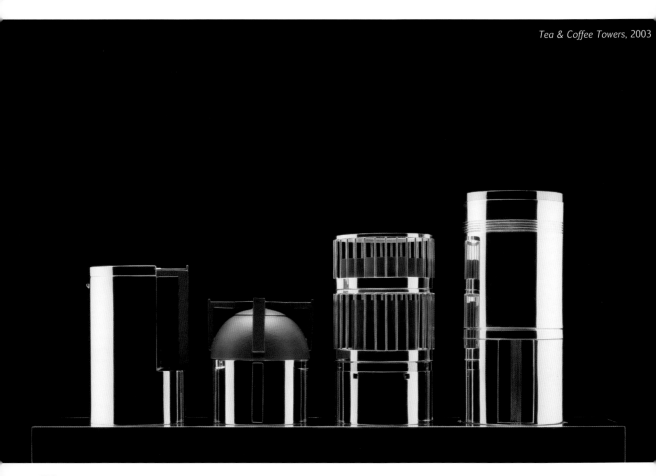

Tea & Coffee Towers, 2003

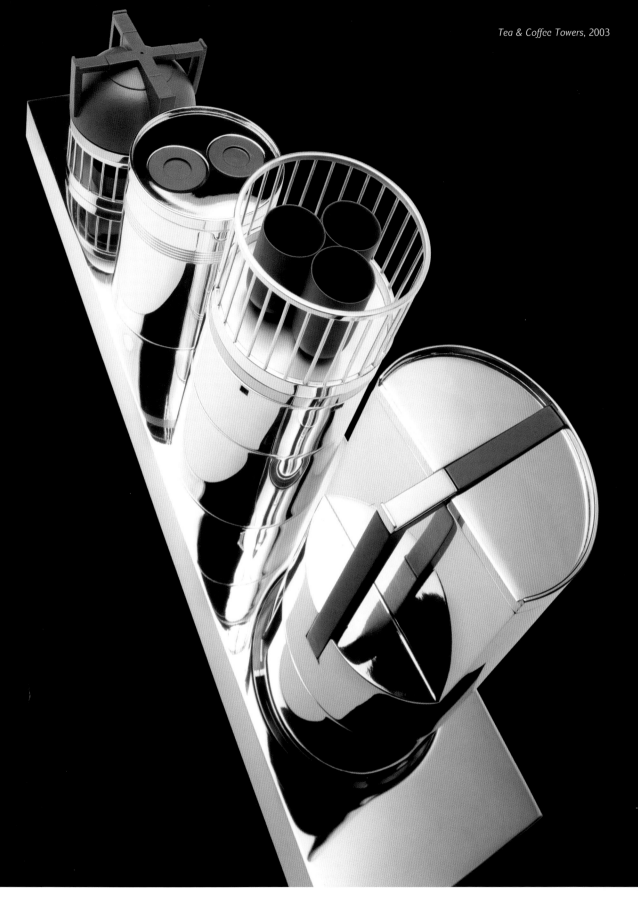

—ALESSANDRO MENDINI

It would be fair to say that Alessi would not be the brand it is today without Alessandro Mendini. As Alessi's general design consultant from 1979, Mendini wears many hats, both professional and personal, when it comes to Alberto Alessi's company and family. Alberto himself reveals, "When people ask me what Mendini does for us, what his role is, I just smile. Alessandro's consulting work covers such a wide range of aspects that his position cannot really be described or even understood by an outsider." At the same time the official chronicler of the company (Mendini is the author of the Paesaggio Casalingo research project), design manager, consultant and journalist, he is also an intimate friend and architect who designed Alberto Alessi's family home, two additions to Alessi's Crusinallo factory, the Alessi Museum as well as Alessi stores around the world. Some of Mendini's most important projects and accomplishments for Alessi include the Anna G., the Tea and Coffee Piazza, the Tea and Coffee Towers and Tendentse.

ALESSI - MENDINI GALAXY

CATALOGUE § HISTORY

BOMBÉ

BOOK

78

80

PAESAGGIO CASALINGO

TIGER MOSCONI

§ 1978 § TRIENNALE HOLLEIN

CONICA ROSSI VENTURI

BOOK

TUSQUET GRAVES

THE AND COFFEE PIAZZA

DECORO NAVONE

BOOK

MEYER

CIBI E RITI

BERLIN

CAFFETTIERA NAPOLETANA

DALISI

BOOK

CINTURA DI ORIONE

SAPPER NOUVEL

STARCK

OFFICINA

FRENCH DESIGN

SOLFERINO

POZAMPARK

ALBERTO'S BOOK

NOT IN PROD. NEXT TO PROD.

SCARZELLA'S BOOK

KING KONG

SOLOVIEW

PAESAGGIO DA CUCINA CON PENTOLE

ASPEN

GIOCO DEI POMOLI

ISOZAKI

PENTOLE FALSTAF

COMPLEMENTI DI ARREDO

CUCINA FORNETTO

MARI BONET CASTIGLIONI

ORTA LAKE

CASA FELICITÀ

90

NEW STAND 1989 MI

PASSERO SOLITARIO

SAX

PERFUME

RAMS

TWERGI

WOOD

GLAS

PLASTIC

TENDENTZE

CERAMICS PORCELAIN

How would you describe Alessi as a client and the way they work with designers?
In my case, the collaboration with Alberto Alessi was soon like working with a good friend. In general, I think that Mr. Alessi's working relationship with his many designers is conducted with methodical precision.

Your relationship with Alessi began in 1977. How has your relationship with Alessi evolved over the years?
We have always had a two-fold approach, with experimental projects on one side and the design of products on the other.

Why do you think Alessi has achieved its success amongst consumers, apart from its popularity amongst designers?
Alessi's success with the public can be ascribed to the heterogeneity of Alessi's products and the feelings of attachment that they generate.

What are your thoughts on the tripartite division of the brand into the exclusive and experimental Officina Alessi, the mid-ranged Alessi and the democratically affordable A di Alessi?
Over time, the classifications have changed regularly in order to rationalise the collection. I think that the latest subdivision satisfies this need.

What are your thoughts on Alessi's perspective of themselves as inheritors of the legacy of Italian design, of being cultural ambassadors rather than a production line?
I have always believed in and worked toward design being a cultural product and not just a commercial one. I believe that Alberto thinks along the same lines.

How do you see yourself, as a designer who has worked with international clients, fitting into such a tradition of Italian design that Alessi embodies?
Alessi is an international industry with Italian DNA. That's how I see myself: my DNA is Italian – Milanese to be precise.

What is your view of the Anna G. corkscrew now, given its phenomenal success and iconic status?
The Anna G. figure practically came about by chance. Of course, I am happy about her success. I like the fact that people enjoy using this friendly object.

How does the Tendentse project articulate Alessi's design philosophy?
In the beginning of the Alessi production, Tendentse was based on a certain character and specific material, which has always given the series special visibility.

What do you think of the espresso cafetiere and its position in 20th century domesticity?
I predict that stovetop espresso makers of the "Moka" type will be around for a long time to come.

Which were the specific aspects of your architectural training that ended up in the design for the Alessi stores?
The Alessi stores are based on a few clearly defined principles: well-displayed merchandise, a setting that is part like a private home and part like a museum, and an interior that is conceived like an art gallery.

What do you think of Alberto championing work that is at the risky borderline of the "possible" and "not possible"?
If you don't explore areas that involve risk and "danger", no interesting results will be obtained.

Anna G., corkscrew, 1994
Alessandro M., corkscrew, 2003

Alessandro M., corkscrew, 2003

—STEFANO GIOVANNONI

After the era of the maestros ruled by Ettore Sottsass, Richard Sapper and Achille Castiglioni, Stefano Giovannoni is one of the most important of the commissioned designers. He began working with Alessi in 1989 with Guido Venturini (under the collective name King Kong Production) to produce the blockbuster Girotondo series, with the cut-out human figures in a chain. This led to the eventual birth of Family Follows Fiction, which defined most of Alessi's output in the 1990s and for which Giovannoni also designed several of the main items, the most representative being the Merdolino toilet brush. Giovannoni's influence and significance with regard to Alessi cannot be overstated. In 2007, he created The Chin Family, a collaboration with the National Palace Museum of Taiwan; followed by OrienTales in 2008, a line of tableware goldfish and birds; and in 2009, the Banana Family of tableware masquerading as monkeys.

How would you describe Alessi as a client and the way they work with designers?
Alessi is a company which expresses the best of Italian design culture. Alberto has a deep respect for the creators and he is able to influence their work without interfering with the development of their ideas. His approach to the improvement of the project has always been open and positive.

Your relationship with Alessi began in 1989. How has your relationship with Alessi evolved over the years, from the 1990s to more recent times?
I was first introduced to Alberto by Alessandro Mendini, and everything started with the Girotondo project. It was a product that went against the tides with respect to the best sellers of Alessi sold at the time – such as the kettles designed by Graves and Sapper and the fruit squeezer by Starck: very expressive and sophisticated objects from a formal point of view. If we had tried to imitate those design maestros, we could only create a bad copy of their works, so we decided to go in a totally opposite direction. Girotondo is a standard and basic tray. Everything was played on the icon of the little man that turned around its edge. The repeated serial icon represents the shape of kids holding their hands and playing ring-a-ring o'roses. The choice of that icon meant the reclamation of a figurative language ever present in our culture like popular culture. The modern movement has confined the figurative in the kitsch sphere. To reclaim the figurative as a means of communication meant abandoning the design culture traditionally linked to the language and its composition in favour of a new culture of communication and consumer goods. Those little men of Girotondo brought a positive message that everybody was able to understand – a girl of 15 years, her mother or even her grandmother. For this reason, Girotondo had achieved much success. Alessi was supposed to sell 5,000 pieces, but in its first year Alessi already sold around 50,000 pieces. Soon after the success of the basket, having sold 100,000 pieces, the Girotondo serviette rings followed with an astounding success of 200,000 pieces sold per year. The family grew with new products and millions and millions of Girotondo were sold; till today more than 7,000,000 of the

Girotondo series were sold, and held a brand-new record in the history of design-oriented companies. I think the Girotondo tray was a key product and turning point for Alessi. There was an Alessi before the Girotondo and another Alessi after it. Since 1989, the collaboration with Alessi has grown, expressing different feelings related to the changing of our society.

What is your view of Alessi as a brand? Why do you think it has achieved its success amongst consumers (apart from popularity amongst designers)?
Alessi is a company that takes care of people's dreams, emotions and desires. With regards to kitchenware and small design objects, Alessi is definitely the leading company and the point of reference worldwide. In the 1990s, plastic products opened the company to a new range of customers. These new products, through their emotional and sensorial appeal, were able to speak directly to people's imaginations and desires.

What are your thoughts on the tripartite division of the brand into the exclusive and experimental (Officina), the mid-ranged (Alessi) and the democratically affordable (A di Alessi)?
Alessi is a brand whose core business is characterised by a traditional material like steel. When I started working with Alessi, my main intention was to democratise the company by enlarging the communication to a new target of customers, especially to the younger generation. Alessi started in 1993 with the operation of FFF (Family Follow Fiction), which was a direct consequence of Girotondo's success. Through the use of plastic material, FFF was first targeted towards a new generation who was looking for a strongly-featured product, in terms of emotional and sensorial faculties, at an affordable price. Plastic products succeeded in speaking directly to young people, and they began to collect these products. At the end of the 1990s, I returned to steel and designed the successful Mama family. For Officina Alessi, the project includes designs that contributes to the image of the Alessi brand, but are not real industrial products.

Alberto has spent his whole career at Alessi exploring the poetic value of objects around us and insisting on the philosophical aspects of the Italian design factory comparing it to the factory line that his other grandfather ran. What are your thoughts on Alessi's perspective of themselves as inheritors of the legacy of Italian design, of being cultural ambassadors rather than a production line?
Alberto Alessi is, in the design world, like Lorenzo de Medici in our Renaissance: a real intellectual, educated and able to understand more than any other professional in his field on how to manage the complex design world, and how to handle the difficult personalities of designers. His approach expresses at best the synergy between design and company. His theories about design having the element of borderline, as well as his formula for success, in which he analyses the parameters of how a product becomes a best-seller, have been fundamental to my training as a designer.

How do you see yourself, as an Italian designer who has worked with international clients, fitting into such a tradition of Italian design that Alessi works from?
I worked with many different designers and companies in Italy and abroad, but my synergy with the Italian business model is by far the most interesting experience for a designer. In the Italian business model, the company will ask the designer to invent a new type of product that would enable them to achieve a market price four or five times higher than the standard price for the same kind of product. If I have to design a plastic breadbin for Alessi, I know that, regardless of the way I design it, it will cost about 50 euros. The designer has to think of an idea or a strategy that enables the product to be sold at that price, within the appropriate system of distribution.

A design-oriented company does not sell its products at high prices to achieve a greater profit margin. On the contrary, a very careful consideration is given to the price. It takes into account the very mechanism of manufacturing and distribution based on limited quantities, the necessity for quality materials and finish, as well as its manufacturing flexibility (the quantity-colours relationship). The hundreds of thousands of units that may be manufactured and sold every year for a designer's creation are still low compared to the millions of units manufactured by mass-production industries. This is why Italian companies have traditionally acknowledged the importance of a designer's work, recognising him with royalties. This attitude of working on all aspects of a design, continuously reinventing object types and strategy, is linked to the excellence and nobility of a creative process that is so deeply rooted in Italian culture and tradition.

The Girotondo man motif is used for the Fiat Panda Alessi. Was this deliberate? What do you think of this motif being representative of the brand?
Of course it was deliberate. The Girotondo became a family that includes 65 products which was representative of the brand.

How do you think Mami fulfils the Alessi credo of a "kind of handicraft made with the help of machines"?
Mami is the icon of the pot. Before starting this project, I discussed with Alberto Alessi deeply on the theory of Heidegger (the German philosopher) about the "thingness of the thing". In this case, we talked about the "potness of the pot", the individuation of the essential characters of the object that, in the memory and in the collective imagination, determined its archetype, which is recognizable to everybody. Mami is not one of many designer pots or pans; it is The Pot. It is the referential product for all kitchenware companies and today, the product has the highest turnover in the Alessi catalogue.

How do the products in plastic (like Lilliput, Fruitmama, Nutty the cracker, Merdolino, OrienTales) continue the tradition of Italian Design in the 1960s which had a strong focus on plastic?
The operation FFF (Family Follow Fiction) became very popular as they relate better to the emotions of younger people, who considered these plastic products as new icons of design. Today a design product, unlike a television program speaking to a large mass of people, has been something for a niche group of intellectual people. For them, quantity and quality are both important points to be reflected in an industrial product. Plastic is an extremely interesting material because of its great flexibilities in creating different shapes, transparencies, textures, and colours. Moreover, its lower price range makes the product accessible to everyone.

What are your thoughts on Alessi moving beyond the kitchen and into the realm of the bathroom with the Il Bagno Alessi projects?
From the Girotondo steel products to the FFF plastics, from the Mami to OrienTales, my work has evolved through different historical periods, relating to different feelings. However, the same intention to move the focus from design to communication still prevail, just as I continue to consider icons, archetypes, memories and imaginations as a main reference in creating objects with the aim of speaking to people.

What is your thinking of Alberto's championing of working at the risky borderline of the "possible" and "not possible"?
In my opinion, a company can sacrifice some investments to produce interesting objects with a strong image, but with a low selling point. In any case, I think creating a strategy that concentrates on producing real industrial best-selling products should be the main focus for every design company.

Babà series, multi-purpose container, kitchen box, bathroom waste bin, stool, laundry basket with lid, 2004

The Chin Family, 2007

SPREADING THE WORD

5

Communication Channels

ADVERTISING

1970s

The most important Alessi advertising campaigns originated in the early 1970s. In the days before digital touch-ups and Photoshop, Alessi's campaigns were highly shaped by what American critic Susan Sontag defines as the photographer's "heroism of vision". The austere photography of Attilio Del Comune and in particular, Aldo Ballo, came to define this era, where their unique sensibilities expressed a vision of the object in its pure and absolute state. Ballo would become one of the most important creators of the Alessi image in a long and lasting collaboration. These early advertising campaigns were part of what critic Isa Vercelloni calls the "sharp, precise and winning image" which propelled the international reputation of Italian design.

1975

"The art of pouring,
with an Alessi signature"

FEATURED: PROGRAMMA 8, TABLE SET,
EIJA HELANDER AND FRANCO SARGIANI,
1975 **AGENCY**: PIRELLA GÖTTESCHE

1976

"Alessi presents an art multiple by
Carmelo Cappello, an art multiple
by Carmelo Cappello, an art
multiple by Carmelo Cappello, an
art multiple by Carmelo Cappello,
an art multiple..."

FEATURED: CIRCULAR HORIZONTAL
SHAPE, NUMBERED EDITION, CARMELO
CAPPELLO, 1976 **PHOTOGRAPHER**: ALDO
BALLO **AGENCY**: PIRELLA GÖTTESCHE

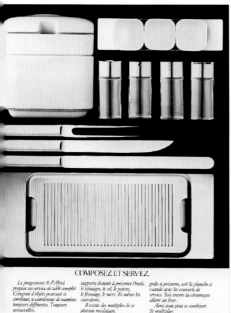

1976

"Compose and serve."

FEATURED: PROGRAMMA 8, TABLE SET,
EIJA HELANDER AND FRANCO SARGIANI,
1975 **AGENCY:** PIRELLA GÖTTESCHE

1976

"And now build a house around it."

FEATURED: TEOREMA, NUMBERED
EDITION, PINO TOVAGLIA, 1976
PHOTOGRAPHY: ALDO BALLO
AGENCY: PIRELLA GÖTTSCHE

1977

"Whether you believe it or not,
this is a basket."

FEATURED: MAYA, NUMBERED EDITION,
GIULIO CONFALONIERI, 1977
PHOTOGRAPHER: ALDO BALLO
AGENCY: PIRELLA GÖTTSCHE

ADVERTISING

1976

"An idea to play with"

FEATURED: 190, SOUP TUREEN,
UFFICIO TECNICO ALESSI, 1964
AGENCY: PIRELLA GÖTTESCHE

1977

"This knife sits in a slot that stays
on a chopping board that goes
into a container that stays on a
tray that stays on another tray
that stays..."

FEATURED: PROGRAMMA 8, TABLE SET,
EIJA HELANDER AND FRANCO SARGIANI,
1975 AGENCY: PIRELLA GÖTTESCHE

1978

"Mix and serve"

FEATURED: PROGRAMMA 8, TABLE SET,
EIJA HELANDER AND FRANCO SARGIANI,
1975 AGENCY: PIRELLA GÖTTESCHE

1979

"Beautility"

FEATURED: PROGRAMMA 8, SALAD
SERVING SET, **AGENCY:** PIRELLA GÖTTSCHE

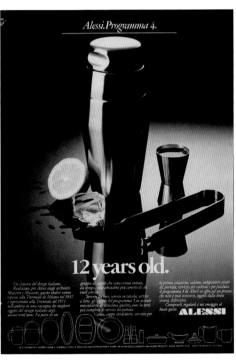

1979

"12 years old."

The 870 cocktail shaker featured
in this advertisement was one of
the first Alessi objects designed by
external designers, Carlo Mazzeri
and Luigi Massoni, in 1957.

FEATURED: 870, COCKTAIL SHAKER,
LUIGI MASSONI AND CARLO MAZZERI,
1957 **AGENCY:** PIRELLA GÖTTESCHE

1979

"A table service so simple to look
complicated."

FEATURED: PROGRAMMA 8,
RECTANGULAR TRAYS, EIJA HELANDER
AND FRANCO SARGIANI, 1975
AGENCY: PIRELLA GÖTTESCHE

1980s

While the advertising campaigns of the 1970s were characterised by Aldo Ballo's rigorous photography, which sought a clarity of the object without distraction, the campaigns of the 1980s register a subtle shift where elements of context and allusions to home and professional use are introduced into the advertising images. The work of Mario Zappalà, one of the greatest exponents of Italian advertising photography in the 1980s, for the campaign Officina Alessi: Art History is made up of acts of disobedience *is hailed as one of the decade's most innovative, investigating new photographic forms and daring compositions. The campaign also encapsulates one of the core tenets of Alessi's philosophy – to create innovative objects and to constantly enrich the playing field of design by encouraging the gifts of the most talented designers, photographers and creative communicators.*

1980

"Composition:"

FEATURED: TRAYS, AA. VV.
AGENCY: PIRELLA GÖTTESCHE

1980

"Wherever you put it, an Alessi object is always in the centre of the house."

FEATURED: 5070, CONDIMENT SET: OIL, VINEGAR, SALT AND PEPPER, ETTORE SOTTSASS, 1978
AGENCY: PIRELLA GÖTTESCHE

**Per chi ha una casa nuova.
O ancora meglio,
per chi ha una casa vecchia.**

Sono tutti in acciaio inossidabile 18/10, sono tutti Alessi. Sono quattro modi, proposti da Alessi, per variare un tema: quello dei contenitori. In quante forme si può piegare l'acciaio inossidabile per farne un vassoio o un cestino?

Forse no. Osservate, per esempio, i quattro oggetti fotografati in questa pagina. L'estremo a destra è un oggetto classico, quasi professionale: la guantiera rotonda disegnata da Ettore Sottsass. Più sotto, un cestino a filo, molto "inventato". In alto, un contenitore traforato, ancora di Sottsass e, a sinistra, un esempio di buon design italiano: Tiffany di Coppola. Uno di questi quattro oggetti, o uno dei tanti altri oggetti Alessi qui non fotografati, è per voi che avete una casa, nuova o vecchia che sia.

In tante, in tante: basta dare uno sguardo al catalogo Alessi per osservare una rassegna di contenitori come nemmeno il più fornito dei negozi può mettere insieme. E ciascuno di questi oggetti dà alla casa un tono particolare, un accento tutto suo. È paradossale dire che chi deve arredare una casa, può cominciare con un vassoio Alessi? E chi, vuole rinnovarla, può farlo a partire da un cestino?

ALESSI

**Un oggetto Alessi,
dovunque lo mettiate,
è al centro della casa.**

LO SHAKER BOSTON, DISEGNATO DA ETTORE SOTTSASS, CON LA CONSULENZA DI ALBERTO GOZZI

1981

"For those who own a new house. Or better still, for those who own an old house."

FEATURED: BASKETS AND TRAYS, AA. VV.
AGENCY: PIRELLA GÖTTESCHE

**Caffettiera Alessi Magnum.
Cioè, non plus ultra.**

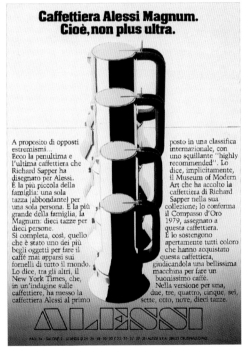

A proposito di opposti estremismi... Ecco la penultima e l'ultima caffettiera che Richard Sapper ha disegnato per Alessi. È la più piccola della famiglia: una sola tazza (abbondante) per una sola persona. E la più grande della famiglia, la Magnum: dieci tazze per dieci persone. Si completa, così, quello che è stato uno dei più begli oggetti per fare il caffè mai apparsi sui fornelli di tutto il mondo. Lo dice, tra gli altri, il New York Times, che, in un'indagine sulle caffettiere, ha messo la caffettiera Alessi al primo posto in una classifica internazionale, con uno squillante "highly recommended". Lo dice, implicitamente, il Museum of Modern Art che ha accolto la caffettiera di Richard Sapper nella sua collezione; lo conferma il Compasso d'Oro 1979, assegnato a questa caffettiera. E lo sostengono apertamente tutti coloro che hanno acquistato questa caffettiera, giudicandola una bellissima macchina per fare un buonissimo caffè. Nella versione per una, due, tre, quattro, cinque, sei, sette, otto, nove, dieci tazze.

ALESSI

1981

"Alessi coffee maker magnum size. That is to say a non plus ultra."

FEATURED: 9090 COFFEE MAKER,
RICHARD SAPPER, 1979
AGENCY: PIRELLA GÖTTESCHE

1982

"Wherever you put it, an Alessi object is always in the centre of the house."

FEATURED: BOSTON, SHAKER,
ETTORE SOTTSASS, 1979
AGENCY: PIRELLA GÖTTESCHE

1982

"This is the knife.
While you see it working, we will
start telling you something about
the spoon and the fork."

FEATURED: DRY CUTLERY SET,
ACHILLE CASTIGLIONI, 1982
AGENCY: PIRELLA GÖTTESCHE

1983

"This is the spoon.
While you see it working, we will
start telling you something about
the knife and the fork."

FEATURED: DRY CUTLERY SET,
ACHILLE CASTIGLIONI, 1982
AGENCY: PIRELLA GÖTTESCHE

1984

"Wherever you put it, an Alessi
object is always in the centre of
the house."

FEATURED: 9091 KETTLE,
RICHARD SAPPER, 1983
AGENCY: PIRELLA GÖTTESCHE

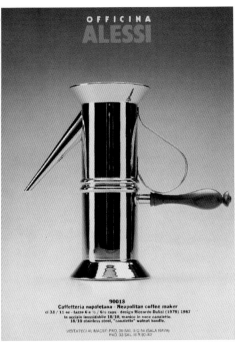

1987

FEATURED: 90018, NEAPOLITAN
COFFEE MAKER, RICCARDO DALISI, 1987
PHOTOGRAPHY: ALDO BALLO

1988

"Art history is made up of acts of disobedience."

Photographer Mario Zappalà, together with Michele Gottsche, created one of Alessi's most intense and caustic campaigns, Officina Alessi: Art history is made up of acts of disobedience.

FEATURED: THE CAMPIDOGLIO,
TRAY, ROBERT VENTURI, 1985
AGENCY: PIRELLA GÖTTESCHE
PHOTOGRAPHER: MARIO ZAPPALÀ

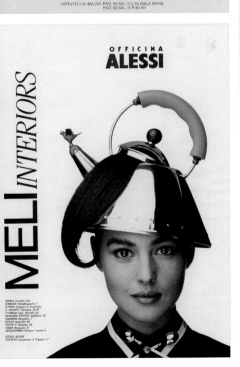

1989

FEATURED: 9091 KETTLE,
RICHARD SAPPER, 1983
AGENCY: PIRELLA GÖTTESCHE

1990s

The beginning of the 1990s heralded a new era of "play" for Alessi. Alessi's philosophy in the 1990s veered towards a more general audience with more accessible and playful products. This was accompanied by marketing conceptualisations that led to the creation of A di Alessi in the 2000s. In the early 1990s a highly successful new venture in plastic was initiated under the label Family Follows Fiction. This was presented as an innovation designed to facilitate collaboration with younger designers, and it has also enabled Alessi to reach a wider market through more affordable goods and a more populist aesthetic. Products in metal continued to be bestsellers – examples include the Juicy Salif, 9091 and Mama-ò.

1990

FEATURED: JUICY SALIF, CITRUS SQUEEZER, PHILIPPE STARCK, 1990
PHOTOGRAPHY: STEFAN KIRCHNER, 1990

1990

FEATURED: COVER OF *TWERGI* CATALOGUE

Alessi, Paesaggio Domestico, *1921-1990. Particolare.*

Da 70 anni Alessi crea e distrugge. Da 70 anni disobbedisce a tutte le regole, a cominciare dalle proprie.
Come in un'avventura senza fine, gli oggetti Alessi hanno costruito un nuovo paesaggio domestico in divenire, e ogni volta l'hanno stravolto, rivoluzionato e ricreato.
Oggi Alessi si getta dietro le spalle 70 anni di glorioso passato e si prepara a partire, ancora una volta, verso un futuro inesplorato.

ALESSI

1991

"Alessi, Domestic Landscape, 1921-1990. Detail."

For the Paesaggio Domestico campaign, Richard Sapper's 9091 kettle was photographed by Carlo Facchini, where a landscape of imaginary buildings appear on the reflective surface of the kettle.

FEATURED: 9091, KETTLE, RICHARD SAPPER, 1983
AGENCY: PIRELLA GÖTTESCHE LOWE

OFFICINA
ALESSI
La Casa della Felicità

"Stehleuchte"
design Aldo Rossi
1991

1991

"Floor lamp."

FEATURED: LAMP, ALDO ROSSI, UNDER LA CASA DELLA FELICITA PROJECT BY ALESSANDRO MENDINI
PHOTOGRAPHY: SANTI CALECA
AGENCY: PIRELLA GÖTTESCHE LOWE

OFFICINA
ALESSI

"Mama-ò"
Horvidor
design Andrea Branzi, 1992

1992

FEATURED: COVER OF *LA CASA DELLA FELICITÀ* CATALOGUE
PHOTOGRAPHY: STEFAN KIRCHNER

1991

"When you realise that Carlo is a cork how will you react?"

FEATURED: CARLO, STOPPER, CSA, MATTIA DI ROSA, 1994
AGENCY: PIRELLA GÖTTESCHE LOWE

1994

FEATURED: ES01, OVEN-TO-TABLE HOLDER, ETTORE SOTTSASS, 1994
AGENCY: SOTTSASS ASSOCIATI

Completo portapirofila in acciaio inossidabile 18/10 con pirofila in porcellana.
Design Ettore Sottsass, 1994

1994

"Alessi express."

FEATURED: COFFEE MAKERS, AA. VV.
PHOTOGRAPHY: CARLO PAGGIARINO
AGENCY: PIRELLA GÖTTESCHE LOWE

1996

"Hang a Philippe Starck in your kitchen."

Jean Baptiste Mondino playfully displays Philippe Starck next to kitchenware.

FEATURED: FAITOO, PHILIPPE STARCK, 1996 **AGENCY:** PIRELLA GÖTTESCHE LOWE, 1996

1997

"Alessi strikes again!"

FEATURED: FAMILY FOLLOWS FICTION, 1990 **AGENCY:** PIRELLA GÖTTESCHE LOWE

1999

"Alessi. Extra ordinary."

FEATURED: MAMI, POTS, STEFANO GIOVANNONI, 1999 **AGENCY:** PIRELLA GÖTTESCHE LOWE

2000s

Alessi's recent advertising campaigns have evolved from the campaigns of the 1990s. Through presenting their products in the unlikeliest of ways, the company's campaigns continue to show how their expressive creations embody a spirit of "play". In these campaigns, all the images are accompanied by the tagline "Alessi. Extra Ordinary.", and the Alessi product is thrust into different imaginative worlds, each object functioning as a visual metaphor. This approach is what Michele Göttsche, the art director for the Alessi campaigns over 20 years, describes as using "photos to tell a series of surreal stories whose protagonist is sometimes a saucepan, sometimes a coffee maker, sometimes a citrus press, sometimes a kettle".

2000

This campaign tells a story of revenge. The sharp blade of a Caccia knife rips through a piece of white canvas. The story lies in the sublime gesture of a slash.

FEATURED: CACCIA, CUTLERY SET, LUGICI CACCIA DOMINIONI-LIVIO AND PIER GIACOMO CASTIGLIONI, 1990
AGENCY: LOWE LINTAS PIRELLA GÖTTESCHE

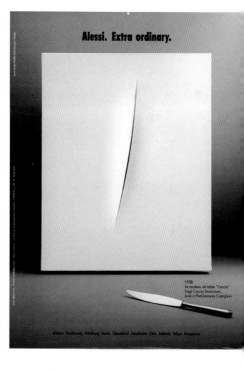

2000

Under Michele Göttsche's art direction, this campaign for Mendini's Anna G. tells a story of metamorphosis. With a simple turn of the skirt upwards, Anna G. becomes a star, Marilyn Monroe-style. In Gottsche's words, "A corkscrew has never been so sexy."

FEATURED: ANNA G., CORKSCREW, ALESSANDRO MENDINI, 1994
AGENCY: LOWE LINTAS PIRELLA GÖTTESCHE

2001

FEATURED: NUOVO MILANO, CUTLERY SET, ETTORE SOTTSASS, 1987
AGENCY: LOWE LINTAS PIRELLA GÖTTESCHE

ADVERTISING

2003

FEATURED: DRY, BAVERO, ORSEGGI
– CUTLERY, TABLE AND GLASS SET,
ACHILLE CASTIGLIONI, 1982-1997
AGENCY: LOWE PIRELLA

2001

FEATURED: 9093 KETTLE,
MICHAEL GRAVES, 1985
AGENCY: LOWE PIRELLA

2001

FEATURED: AC04,
FRUIT BOWL/COLANDER,
ACHILLE CASTIGLIONI, 1995
AGENCY: LOWE PIRELLA

2003

FEATURED: MAMI, PRESSURE COOKER,
STEFANO GIOVANNONI, 2003
AGENCY: LOWE PIRELLA

La tavola di Achille Castiglioni
1997

Alessi. Extra ordinary.

Milano Düsseldorf Berlin Hamburg London Stockholm Oslo Helsinki Tokyo San Francisco Atlanta Barcelona Paris

"Blow up
Portaagrumi in acciaio inossidabi
design Fratelli Campan
200

Alessi. Extra ordinary.

Milano Paris Berlin Düsseldorf Hamburg München London Stockholm Oslo Helsinki Tokyo Singapore New York Atlanta Chicago San Francis

2003

FEATURED: ALESSI, 2003
AGENCY: LOWE PIRELLA

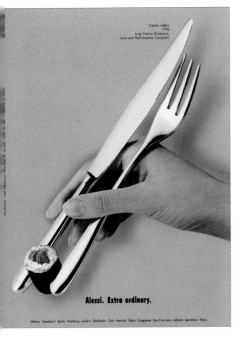

2003

FEATURED: CACCIA, CUTLERY SET,
LUGICI CACCIA DOMINIONI-LIVIO AND
PIER GIACOMO CASTIGLIONI, 1990
AGENCY: LOWE PIRELLA

2003

FEATURED: 370, CITRUS BASKET,
UFFICIO TECNICO ALESSI, 1952
AGENCY: LOWE PIRELLA

2007

Delicately arranged, a set of cutlery
and plates forms the image of a
flower, like a work of art.

FEATURED: COLOMBINA COLLECTION,
TABLE, CUTLERY AND GLASS SET, DORIANA
AND MASSIMILIANO FUKSAS, 2007
AGENCY: LOWE PIRELLA FRONZONI

WONDER STORES

According to Paolo Cravedi, managing director of Alessi USA, "People fall in love with this space. It's wonderful to see the fascination and glee on people's faces as they enter the store and embark on a journey of emotions and memories rekindled by our fine design". "Here" refers to Alessi's flagship store on Greene Street in New York's SoHo district. And fine design, a marriage of sophisticated technology and sterling craftsmanship, is exactly what Alessi is known for. Hani Rashid, when appointed as designer for the store, bore that in mind when he came up with the concept for the former antique store. Collaborating with lighting designers Tillotson Design Associates, he utilised lighting and sculpture to highlight the display of Alessi's products. The result is a gem of a store which bedazzles. Literally. Nine 18-inch-wide bands form incandescent ribbons of white light that run up the north wall of the store and traverse the length of the ceiling. Already eye-catching and experimental, Rashid also had to combine these with other lighting elements to work with the asymmetrical and narrow (65-feet-long by 19-feet-wide) spatial dimensions. Reflective surfaces such as mirrored walls and high-gloss paint enhance the gleaming feel while ceiling clusters of light fixtures were carefully placed to draw attention to the products without a blinding glare. A Tarallucci e Vino coffee outlet takes up the anterior of the store. A first for an Alessi store, the bar serves its famous coffee in Alessi espresso cups, glassware and vessels.

FLAGSHIP STORE,
—NEW YORK

130 Greene St,
10012 New York,
United States

Your collaboration with Tillotson Design Associates resulted in a unique store where light was both an instrument and a material for the walls. What made you decide to use light this way?
In all our work, light is pivotal to the forms, spatial aspects, and so on, which make architecture "work". I came to architecture through film and photography where light was, and still is, the key to those mediums' effectiveness and power. In architecture, using light is the way in which I carve and form space. Tillotson was a great facilitator for this in the Alessi store, as the company's technical knowledge and ideas were in tandem with our vision for the space and its presence and function as not only a viable store but an installation work set into a Manhattan block in SoHo.

Did you ever fear it would be too harsh or make for an uncomfortable buying experience?
On the contrary, people take to space when it is dramatic and well thought out as this one is. I have heard that this store is Alessi's number one retail venue in the world and, despite a horrible economy at the moment, I attribute that to the architecture being captivating, strong and curious – light form and mathematics have a lot to do with that.

Which aspect of the brand or its products led to you deciding to manipulate lighting elements in the SoHo store?
Actually lighting in all our work, as I have said, is important and key. In terms of this store, the idea that objects are, for the most part, made from metals and plastics that reflect and play with light, was something we thought was especially interesting. The lighting design we made for the shelving, which was done in collaboration with Visplay, was precisely formulated with special spectral effects to highlight the objects, their curvatures and colour, all integral things to the Alessi brand and its products.

The coffee bar is, famously, a first for Alessi stores worldwide. What inspired that?
In my discussions with Alberto and Jan in New York I had suggested that as a way to bring other sensory aspects from the Italian landscape to the store. The store design is predicated on a mathematical outlay of the Lago d'Orta and Maggiore region and, to offset the mathematical purity of that interpretation, we thought the sound and smells of espresso and the conversations that accompany that would be a great addition to the mise-en-scène and experience of this small work of architecture.

Were there specific aspects of your interest in virtual architecture that ended up in the design for the physical store? Can the Alessi flagship store be called a fusion of the virtual and the physical?
Yes, very much, in interpreting the landscapes and beauty of the north of Italy. We mapped that into computer models that then allowed us to experiment with form, light and movement. The resulting light bands, architectural work, colour, and so on, came from these virtual studies and meditations. Entering the store is, in a sense, entering into an augmented reality caught between New York City and the northern Italian lakes and mountains where the Alessi brand was born.

You've constantly stressed the need for architecture to be for people. ("Our buildings are made for people, not for other architects" – interview with Archidea) and you've also spoken of the need to have an experience, a real discovery that people can get immersed in. How, in your opinion, has the SoHo store achieved this?
The store is a model architecture for larger urban spaces and thinking. From the entry, the coffee bar and small museum-like space at the front, to the full experience of the products, shelving, and so on, the store is a journey through artefacts by and from architects and designers as things you can control, touch and adore. This is analogous to city space in my mind – we meander through streets and buildings in search of experience and profound interfaces and we, as architects, believe that can be provoked, if not designed. The store provides a suspended condition of viewing, appreciating, holding, and, perhaps, acquiring. It marries what we seek from museums and galleries coupled with the visceral need to consume and take things away as mementos or gifts or, more importantly, as conquests. The Alessi store was, for us, the outcome of the immense respect we have for a company that holds, above all else, a belief in design, aesthetics and culture as a way in which to navigate life, cities and the being. The store's architecture is a reflection of those tenets and criteria for experience and the future of cities and architecture.

Hani Rashid

Tigrito, Miriam Mirri, 2005

ALESSI SHOP,
—HAMBURG

Neuer Wall 55
0354 Hamburg
Germany

Following his successful design of Alessi stores in the
United States, New York City-based Hani Rashid turns to
Europe with another accomplishment for the brand, this
time as architect and designer of the Alessi shop in the
German city of Hamburg.

The full length four-metre-high glass front effectively
puts the space on display. As with several other Alessi
stores around the world, retail items are arranged as
in a museum space, for the perusal of customers and
in line with the Alessi philosophy of designing objects
that transcend their mere function in the kitchen. They
become objet d'art, studies in poetry and beauty.

A clear divide is at work at the Hamburg store – upon
entering, customers encounter the left side of the shop,
clad in a milky coloured wall covering of pixel graphic
art. This forms the backdrop of an area set aside for
exhibiting items from the Officina Alessi range. The other
side of the 80-square-metre space is a contrast in colour
and surface. Here, what dominate are high gloss orange
glass tops and a wall installation combined with a matte
black finish on the rest of the wall and flooring. Located
right in the city centre, the Hamburg store promises to be
yet another dynamic retail space in the tradition of Alessi
wonder stores.

SHOP MUSEUM —PARIS

31, Boulevard Raspail
75007 Paris
France

Alberto Alessi recalls his first meeting with Martí Guixé in 1998, "Fernando Amat advised me to invite him to spend a week in Crusinallo to see if we could transform into mass-produced industrial products some of his quite amazing and brilliant, if paradoxical, designs. Back then nothing concrete emerged from the collaboration, but since then I've nurtured the hope of doing something together. And that opportunity arrived when we needed to design the second Alessi shop in Paris … this time on the Rive Gauche."

A fortuitous event, as it turned out to be. The second flagship store in Paris, on Boulevard Raspail, two minutes from the Metrò Rue du Bac and the shopping area of Boulevard Saint-Germain feeds into the quirky, bohemian vibe of the left bank. The façade of the 19th century space is a 1950s shade of cherry red, an introduction to the bright red lacquer that borders the bottom of all the walls around the store, a charming, almost vintage touch that works with the wood parquet flooring and plain white walls.

Designed by Barcelona and Berlin-based designer Martí Guixé, the shop is fronted by a five-metre-long full-length store window revealing cantilever shelves, on which are placed the Alessi merchandise. Guixé has preserved the original floor plan with corridors that narrow and widen as customers move to the back of the shop. Winding through the 80-square-metre space inspecting the items, is an experience akin to visiting exhibited displays in a museum. Indeed, this Parisian flagship store is also called the Alessi Shop Museum.

Speaking of the bold colour and fanciful illustration on the shop's glass front and interior walls, Alberto praises the design as "a great attempt to show the great panoply of our products in another light, with a dash of the quirky humour that is his trademark".

ALESSI SHOP
—TOKYO

3-2-5 Kita-Aoyama,
Minato-Ku,
107-0061 Tokyo,
Japan

Drawing by Alessandro Mendini

ALESSI
AT THE
MUSEUM

UNITED STATES: (1) SFMOMA – San Francisco Museum of Modern Art, San Francisco | (2) Denver Art Museum, Denver | (3) Minneapolis Institute Of Art, Minneapolis | (4) Philadelphia Museum of Art, Philadelphia | (5) MoMA – The Museum of Modern Art, New York | (5) Smithsonian – Cooper-Hewitt, National Design Museum, New York | (5) The Metropolitan Museum of Art, New York | **ICELAND:** (6) MUDESA – The Icelandic Museum of Design and Applied Art, Reykjavik | **UNITED KINGDOM:** (7) Design Museum, London | (7) Victoria & Albert Museum, London | **BELGIUM:** (8) Design Museum, Ghent | **FRANCE:** (9) Centre Pompidou, Paris | (9) Musee Des Arts Decoratifs, Paris | **THE NETHERLANDS:** (10) Stedelijk Museum, Amsterdam | (11) Groninger Museum, Groningen | **GERMANY:** (12) Museum Für Angewandte Kunst, Cologne | (13) Museum Für Angewandte Kunst, Frankfurt | (14) Die Neue Sammlung, Munich | (15) Neue Sächsische Galerie, Chemnitz | **SPAIN:** (16) Museu d'Arts Decoratives de Barcelona, Barcelona | **SWITZERLAND:** (17) Museum Für Gestaltung, Zurich | **ITALY:** (18) La Triennale Di Milano, Milan | **AUSTRIA:** (19) MAK, Museum Für Angewandte Kunst, Vienna | **DENMARK:** (20) Louisiana Museum of Modern Art, Humlebaek | **NORWAY:** (21) Museum of Applied Art, Oslo | **FINLAND:** (22) Design Museum, Helsinki | **ISRAEL:** (23) The Israel Museum, Jerusalem | **BRAZIL:** (24) Museu De Arte, São Paulo | **AUSTRALIA:** (25) National Gallery of Victoria, Melbourne | (26) The Australian National Gallery, Canberra | (27) Powerhouse Museum, Sydney.

INDEX

f

g

h

i

k

l

INDEX

ACKNOW-LEDGEMENTS

We would like to thank all who have contributed in one way or another in the making of this book, especially Francesca Appiani, Daniela Zilocchi, Marina Zanetta and all others at Alessi who have provided us with help every time we asked for it.

Thanks also to the designers and architects who have taken the time to answer our questions for the interview section, and to those who have helped in the arrangements.

Finally, special thanks to Chiara, who has been there every step of the way, for all she has done and for being such a dear person.